'PUT IT DOWN ON PAPER'

The Words and Life of Mary Folsom Blair

A Fifty-Year Search

'PUT IT DOWN ON PAPER'

The Words and Life of Mary Folsom Blair

A Fifty-Year Search

PHIL PRIMACK

LP

Loom Press
Amesbury, Massachusetts
2022

'Put It Down on Paper'
The Words and Life of Mary Folsom Blair: A Fifty-Year Search
Copyright © 2022 by Phil Primack

ISBN 978-0-931507-26-7

Printed in the United States of America
First edition

Design: Victoria Dalis & Hernan Florez
Typefaces: Bebas Kai, EB Garamond, LTC Bodoni, and Proxima Nova Condensed
Author photograph: Frank Siteman

The writings of Mary Folsom Blair are used with the permission of her family.

Cover and frontispiece: Mary Folsom writes in her journal under Arcady's pines
in a photograph c. 1913.

Loom Press
15 Atlantic View
Amesbury, Massachusetts 01913
www.loompress.com
info@loompress.com

For Nancy

Contents

List of Photographs

Mary and Me

Mary just wouldn't let me go.

For nearly a half century, I pursued this woman who was just a name on a real estate listing I first saw in 1974. Mary Evelyn Folsom Blair had died the year before at the age of ninety-one and her property, including an old farmhouse on sixty-four acres of land in the southeastern New Hampshire town of Epping, was for sale.

I cared little about who had lived in that house, let alone who might have wandered the trails behind it, when I fought swarms of mosquitoes on a muggy summer day for my first foray into Mary Folsom Blair's domain. Searching for a spot deep in the woods to build a little house, I tramped through thick forest and past rows of stone walls, New England's Sphinx-like sentries that mark pastures lost to trees competing for space and sky in the arboreal cycle. I came to a creek that bisected the forest, which in the late afternoon was a palette of greens and shadows and rippled sun. Though close to a busy road, the woods were silent, save for nature's calling card of water over stones. Seven decades earlier, standing in what was likely the same spot, Mary Folsom felt that same silence.

"I caught myself listening for a voice, and I heard—oh, well, I heard that voice of which the poet speaks 'Whilst from all around, earth, and her waters, and the depths of air comes a still voice,'" she wrote in 1906, quoting William Cullen Bryant. "It is in the heart of the woods where that 'still voice' is clearest."

Mary was twenty-five when she wrote those words. I was the same age when I first heard that still voice.

I bought the property, though to afford it I had to sell off the old house with ten acres, keeping the remaining land. I found a house site overlooking that creek and began exploring the woods, camping on the land between my stints working on a traveling carnival midway to subsidize the meager wages of freelance writing.

Mary E. Folsom Blair was still just a name on legal papers, but I soon began to hear things about her. Interesting woman. Quite a teacher. Real nature lover. Active Quaker. As a journalist by both profession and mindset, I smelled a good story, one with an unusually personal angle. Little did I know that I would spend decades chasing it down.

Born in 1881 in Epping, Mary is buried in the nearby Friends cemetery that holds generations of her Folsom and maternal Bickford ancestors. Lying next to her is Mary's husband, Edmond G. Blair, whom she met while ice skating when she was thirty-four and convinced of a "spinster" fate. Down the road from the cemetery is the West Epping Friends Meeting House. Mary proudly traced her ancestry to her great grandfather, Joshua Folsom, the first Quaker in Epping in 1742. More than two centuries later, Mary was the last Quaker in town, a legacy she became determined to reverse.

Around the corner from the Meeting House is the former schoolhouse Mary attended as a girl and where her own teaching career began when she was nineteen in 1901. Mary taught in other schools in both New Hampshire and Massachusetts, but despite vowing to never again set foot in West Epping after a miserable first year of teaching, she ended her long classroom career in this white frame building, spending decades educating and shaping children from her community in and beyond the classroom walls.

Her innovative pedagogy included leading straggling parades of boys and girls through miles of forest pathways and roads to her lakeside bungalow, offering impromptu lessons about geography, history, and nature along the way. Even on inside days, Mary often sent students outdoors to do their lessons. During hot weather, she had them go home for bathing suits. "School's in session at the swimming hole," she wrote on the blackboard. Educators would eventually give her approach a label: "Classroom without walls."

Long before government hot lunch programs, Mary kept a kettle of stew on the schoolhouse wood stove to feed Depression-era children. Hungry students, she knew, do not learn. In her annual school registers, some of which I found buried in boxes in former jail cells in the basement of Epping Town Hall, Mary recorded student absences due to, among other reasons, smallpox and other diseases, caring for sick parents, "lack of shoes," "had to milk cows," and "wagon broke down."

The schoolhouse became both a mirror and foundation of Mary's rural community. She and her students produced historical pageants that became major local events. A 1941 bi-centennial production featured a cast of nearly two hundred and drew 4,500 people to a nearby campground. In 1944, the British Broadcasting Company taped Mary's students performing a Thanksgiving play written by their teacher, transmitting their New England words and voices to a worldwide radio audience.

As a child, and decades later as the adult teacher, Mary, who never drove a car, walked to her schoolhouse from her Folsom homestead—the house I briefly owned—a half mile down the road. When I bought the house, it was empty, except for a few pieces of broken furniture and odd items, such as a single old-style skate. (Was she wearing it during her first journal entry about skating miles to Vermont or, decades later, when she met "the Hero"?). I found a few old magazines in the attic—a 1901 *Saturday Evening Post*, a 1922 issue of *Farm and Fireside*, a *Literary Digest* from 1928—but little else. No crinkled letters under the floorboards. No books, no photos, no real evidence of the family who lived in this house built by Mary's father in 1870. Shortly after Mary died in 1973, the house's contents disappeared, most of it given to an auctioneer to sell or discard.

As I kept picking up bits and pieces, I became more interested in this woman who, though childless herself (cruel and unfair fate, she felt), influenced generations of children. Mary came to remind me of a babysitter I had as a boy in the late 1950s whose idea of child care was to send me off into the nearby woods around Round Pond in my hometown of Haverhill, Mass. (about twenty miles from Epping) to look for this butterfly or that tadpole. Those boyhood explorations shaped my desire to live deep in nature.

I was able to satisfy that craving on Mary's land. After building my little house above the creek in the early 1980s, I wanted to know more about Mary. I interviewed relatives, former students, and others. They vividly recalled this determined teacher of words and nature. I learned that she was a pioneer in the movement to get young people engaged with nature, starting with her work with Camp Fire Girls in Massachusetts and continuing with outdoor advocacy in New Hampshire, where she became her county's longest serving 4-H club leader.

Their classroom years with Mary, those hikes through the woods, those nights camping at her bungalow shaped their lives, former students told me. Few of them knew that their former teacher was also quite a writer.

Madelyn Williamson, an Epping historian, gave me my first key lead in 1982. As Mary's family home was emptied, a neighbor managed to salvage two hand-written journals, the diaries of a girl and woman "known on a time as Mary E.," as the twenty-two year-old author dubbed herself in an August 31, 1902, entry. That neighbor gave them to Williamson, who lent them to me. I read the penciled, then inked, pages in a single sitting. I was hooked not only by the words but by the author's story.

The first entries, begun in 1897 when Mary was fifteen, reflect the carefree life of a teenager enjoying a stream of social events ("I had a partner for every dance and danced them all but two."). Her early writing reveals an articulate young soul beginning to evolve but as Mary grows and life becomes more complex, the words are more reflective, at times dark and bitter. The early deaths due to disease of two girlhood classmates as well as her sister upend Mary's comfortable world and shakes her faith. Occasional melancholy and bitterness about "the pain and sorrow this old world holds for a woman" clash with Mary's humor and sharp wit. Failed relationships leave her embittered by "a world full of gay deceivers." Challenges to her classroom ways—many of them decades ahead of the school hierarchy and norms of the era—gnaw at her.

Aware of her shifting moods, Mary turned to her journal as confessor and confidante. "With me, discontent with my own lot, anger because I can not do the things I would and have to do the thing that I would not, covers such a pit of darkness that I am half afraid to take the lid off and look within," she wrote in 1904. Mary sometimes called out her gloominess, and the clouds would break. "I feel better than I did last time I wrote," she penned. "Self reproach has got thru stalking round and thumping me every time she gets a chance." Mary's humor would again shine, often in snippets about new acquaintances ("I shut up one ear when he begins to talk till I know whether I'd better close both.").

Mary had only a high school education—her one year of college did not come until 1916, when she was thirty-five—but she drew from a deep reservoir of learning about literature, history, nature, mythology, and poetry. She absorbed knowledge from everything and everyone, whether books or walks or the quirks and behaviors of those around her. And she thrilled in sharing that knowledge with the young people she taught. "It is a joy that the world holds so much of the unknown," she wrote in 1909. "No matter how long I live, how much I learn, still before me is the lure of the unknown."

Mary entered adulthood as the "New Woman" began to emerge. "By the last decades of the nineteenth century, unexpected and unprecedented changes and opportunities had altered the facts of women's lives," writes Loralee MacPike in a 1989 paper for the *National Women's Studies Association Journal*. Less restricted by Victorian norms, this New Woman could imagine and even pursue a life beyond the confines of domesticity and family, MacPike continues. "Increased access to the work of the world of course required increased physical freedom to move in that world."

Mary's journals capture her transitional time—outings with men and women, rides on her "wheel" or bicycle, attending theater, meeting new people, and, of course, working as a teacher.

Like many other late nineteenth-century women, Mary used her journal to help navigate the changing world. Women, writes Judy Simons in an essay in *Inscribing the Daily, Critical Essays on Women's Diaries*, "use the personal journal to establish for themselves a literary space in which to negotiate versions of selfhood that both trouble and attract them." Mary's journals track her growth and self-discovery as she raises questions and expresses thoughts otherwise kept private from society and certainly from her family. "I've found it best to tie my feelings up in a bundle and store them away and then everything is all serene," she wrote in 1906.

Daily events triggered deep feelings. She recalled the happiness of a nighttime canoe ride through "moist, sweet smelling air [along] the foggy, far off shore half seen through sleep weighted eyelids" but she also recorded the despair of romance foiled. "One may be good friends with a man, chums, comrades, as much as you please, but look out for that element of the personal. It means singed fingers for some poor mortal."

As she finished the second volume of her journals on August 24, 1908, Mary offered a fitting coda. "Well, journal dear, your pages have told or rather listened to many a tale of joy and few of woe." But then came a single-word next line: "Keep" . . . .

Keep what? Keep on with those last thoughts? Keep awake? It seemed very un-Mary for this thoughtful and consistent writer to close on such an unfinished note. My reporter bones kept twitching. I asked around about more Mary writings. Some people believed letters and other material, maybe even more journals, had been in the house. So-and-so might have the stuff, said several so-and-so's, often naming each other.

Needing to focus on my freelance work and the book I was writing about New England country fairs, I eased off my Mary travels. The journals stayed on a shelf, but their author would not. I continued to track down former students, 4-H contemporaries, Quakers, and others. As I kept getting closer to knowing this woman, Mary's words became more resonant to my own life.

I'd marvel at her literary skills, wishing I could compose phrases as sweet as those she used in a letter about her Christmas decorations. "Over the windows are pine boughs bringing the spicy breath of the forests into the house and making quite a festive appearance tied up with streamers of red." As I got to know her former woods, I realized I was walking the same paths wandered and written about by Mary, such as the grove where, in 1906, "the hemlocks stood so thickly and were so weighted down with snow that it seemed like some dim mysterious pagan temple where gods might whisper in my ear some message."

Of all unlikely things, a gravel pit prompted me to get more serious not only about the property but Mary. In the mid-1980s, the people to whom I sold her former house and ten acres sold to a developer who intended to strip the land for gravel. I thought I'd prevented such a possibility with deed restrictions to limit the land to residential or agricultural use only but my lawyer screwed up, leaving a loophole through which a bulldozer eventually tore down the house in which Mary lived most of her life.

Seeing that former Folsom property ripped up made me more determined to protect the land I now owned—and to resume my hunt for Mary. I accomplished the former by granting a conservation easement to what is now the Southeast Land Trust of New Hampshire, forever protecting the remaining land from development. More difficult was tracking down more about Mary, especially additional writings that I was convinced were out there somewhere.

The skeleton key to Arcady

I went back to Richard Hunt Perry.

Born in 1903, he was Mary's nephew and became an executor of her estate. I met Mr. Perry—he was such a proper, reserved Yankee that, despite his urging, I could never get myself to call him by his first name—when we signed papers in 1974. I basically forgot about him until, not even sure he was still alive, I dialed his number nearly two decades later.

Yes, he vaguely remembered me, Mr. Perry answered from his home in Bristol, not too far from Charlestown, N.H., where he was born and where Mary began her journal while living there with her sister, his mother. No, he had no other writing by Mary, but of course I could drop by. We had a good visit in the autumn of 1993, with Mr. Perry sharing some photographs and family history. Just before I left, he asked whether I knew about the "camp" on Pawtuckaway Lake in Nottingham, N.H., a few miles northwest of Epping.

I did recall references to such a place in the journals and some of Mary's former students mentioned it, but that was about all. Mr. Perry recounted childhood visits to the cabin, the walls of which, he said, were covered with names, poems, and other inscriptions left over many decades by Mary and her visitors, including honeymooning former students to whom she lent the camp. He said he believed Mary had sold it to a woman with whom she taught, though he couldn't recall her name. He wondered whether the old bungalow, which Mary christened "Arcady," still stood. I was already wondering the same thing.

Deed research showed that Mary sold the cabin to Pearl Marston, the oldest daughter of a schoolmate with whom Mary boarded while both were in secondary school. Mary and Pearl became lifelong friends and decades later, Pearl became the teacher in the second room of Mary's West Epping Rural School. When age made it too hard for her to maintain the old place, Mary decided to sell Arcady to Pearl, who in turn passed the lakeside bungalow to her daughter, Janice Marston Jassmond.

Janice remembered Mary well and, intrigued by my quest, was happy to show me Arcady. On a bitterly cold day, I drove down rutted White's Grove Road to meet her and her husband Bill at Arcady. The small, sagging structure of rough-sawn boards seemed as out of context from the bigger, newer houses that now crowd Pawtuckaway Lake as the jet skis that attack the quiet like gigantic mechanical mosquitoes.

Using a skeleton key, Janice opened the door. I was transported back a century. Mr. Perry was right. Inscriptions covered the two main doors and the inside walls. Some of them were in Mary's hand; some were scratched in by others as far back as 1908. On the main door to the lake, a barely readable inscription from 1911 listed "the small Perrys," meaning a young Richard Hunt Perry and his brother. Many years later, Mr. Perry's failing eyes lit up when he returned to Arcady and spotted that written link to his childhood.

Tall trees, descendants of the original "mast pines" grown to outfit the King's ships, surround Arcady. Many had snapped in two or fallen, somehow sparing the fragile building below. Maybe Arcady really was guarded by Pan, the Greek god of the wild about whom Mary wrote an epic poem both in her journal and onto a wall. Pan's mythological home was Arcadia, the likely and fitting source for the bungalow's name. Here is where Mary, in a canoe with the special woman she dubbed Anne of Arcady, would listen to "the myriad tongues of that strange world that's hidden to day-time folk and quiet keepers by their own hearth side."

Janice invited me to return when it was less frigid. Then she asked whether I had spoken to Jean Pye.

The next lead.

Mary lived with Jean Pye, the niece of Mary's husband, for about a year before her death in 1973. Jean too was intrigued by my quest and invited me to visit her in Connecticut, where we talked about her Uncle Edmond and Mary. As I was about to leave, Jean asked if I wanted to go through some boxes Mary had left behind. One box was full of letters to Mary. They spanned decades, from gossip-filled notes from girlhood friends to more than a hundred love letters from husband-to-be Edmond. The best treasure was buried at the bottom: Books three and four of the journals of Mary Evelyn Folsom Blair.

1. Two of Mary's journals

I thought that I had finally closed the circle, from a name on a property listing, to Mary's woods, to former students and friends, to Arcady, to Mr. Perry, to a Hartford suburb and the rest of Mary's journals. By the early 1980s, my book about New England country fairs had received good reviews, if lousy sales. Now I was ready to write one about Mary. I had her journals, I'd interviewed people who knew her, and I'd explored Arcady. Some journalists I knew at *Chronicle*, a television news magazine produced by Boston's WCVB-TV, became interested in my Mary saga, leading to an episode about Mary and me that aired on September 29, 2000. The broadcast included footage of former students and others talking about Mary in front of their old school, inside the West Epping Friends Meeting House, and at Arcady.

I'd hoped the *Chronicle* piece might draw interest from a publisher but neither it nor a folder full of query letters I sent generated much response. I moved on to other work and projects, putting the journals and that box of letters back on the shelf. Years passed. Many of the people who knew Mary and helped guide my search died. My interview notes and memories began to fade. Mary had a story to tell, but I simply lacked the discipline to write it.

Finding Anne Reed

Then mortality got on my case. As I turned seventy in 2018, life's loose ends loomed, and Mary was a big one. Pandemic-induced confinement a year later got me to finally dig deeper into that box of letters Jean Pye gave me. I also returned several times to Arcady to ponder the fading script on its walls. Just under that "small Perrys" inscription on the door is another "joyfully begun" in 1912, where Mary wrote onto the dark wood the name of Anne Reed, "who squeaks when she wakes up."

Anne Reed was a central figure in Mary's life. The first journal reference to her was in 1910, with Mary writing that she found "much consolation in Anne Reed." By then, Mary had decided not to further pursue things with two men with whom she had considered "playing partners." And before Anne, Mary had been betrayed by another woman to whom she had become very close. "I cut her dead," Mary wrote of that woman, but Anne Reed was a very different matter. Mary still wanted her in her life even when, four years after being dubbed "Anne of Arcady," Anne became "Anne of Arkansas," moving to that faraway state with one of Arcady's "Gentle Knights of the Tent and Ashen Blade," as Mary termed the men who camped out at Arcady.

Mary struggled to find what today we might call a soul mate. In 1913, when she was thirty-two, Mary confided to her journal her doubts about ever finding one. "Well, I'm going alone—my own road—alone." A year later, still feeling wounded, Mary filled nearly half of the brown notebook that was the third volume of her journal with a "strange sort of an engagement present" for Anne. It was in the form of a long letter and poems that wistfully, and painfully, recalled their intimate times together.

Was this anguished message of love and loss ever sent? I wondered. I was intrigued by the close bonds between Mary and Anne and Marian earlier. Maybe her experiences with those women, combined with her oft-stated fear of becoming a "spinster," made Mary more open to Edmond Blair when he skated into her life in 1915.

Edmond showered Mary with letters of love and devotion. "I was made and want to look for you, and wait for you, and become yours forever," was typical of his sentiments, which she shared, despite differences in age and religion. (He was six years younger and a devout

French-Canadian Catholic to her long Yankee Quaker lineage.). After a courtship that was intense but often long-distance because of work, the two wed in 1918 in a Catholic Church ceremony. None of Mary's family or friends attended.

Even after they were each married and far apart geographically, Mary and Anne maintained their closeness. Who was this woman? With such a common maiden name and no address more specific than Arkansas, my hope to learn more about Anne Reed seemed futile. Once again, I thought I was done connecting the dots of Mary's life. But then, deep in that box of letters, I found a single yellowed envelope with the return address of a Pine Bluff, Ark., business. With the help of my good friends Google and Ancestry.com, I located Anne Reed's great grandson in nearby Durham, N.H. More than a century after Mary first inscribed "Anne Reed" on the bungalow door, I brought him and his mother— Anne Reed's granddaughter—back to Arcady.

Like a meandering trail through the forest, that is the long path to the words and life recounted here. As much as possible, the first two parts of this book keep to the chronology of Mary's first two journals, Book I (1897-1902) and Book II (1902-1908). The section on Mary's relationships is based on the journals, letters to and from Mary, and recollections of others.

"I want to talk to someone dreadfully," Mary wrote when she was twenty-one. "I want to see the pros and cons set down like little tin warriors in a mimic battle. And there is no one that I can or will talk to. Shall I put it down on paper? Yes I will. It may be that I shall regret putting anything down in black and white for folks to read when I am dust and ashes."

I do not think that Mary would regret the words and life put down here.

—Phil Primack
February 2022

Part One
The Early Journals

All excerpts from journals and letters appear as they were written,
including grammar, spelling, and punctuation. Ellipses indicate where
text has been edited. Dates for letters refer to their postmarks.

"PUT IT DOWN ON PAPER"

Chapter 1

"A contrast between what I wanted and what is within my reach."

"Journals seem to be the order of the day or perhaps I should say the order of the year," fifteen-year-old Mary Evelyn Folsom writes as she joins friends of hers already following that order. "I am anxious to see how long I shall keep it up."

Mary Evelyn Folsom, also known as May or M.E., was born on July 8, 1881, in Epping, New Hampshire, the youngest of the five children of Thomas Charles Folsom and Mary Bickford Folsom. Mary's forebears tended to live long lives, as she would herself; people who knew her said Mary's own and her inherited recollections spanned the arc of American history, from just after the American Revolution through the presidency of Richard M. Nixon.

Mary's great grandfather, Joshua Folsom, was born in 1721 and came to Epping in 1741, the same year that the town, which had been part of colonial Exeter, N.H., was incorporated. Joshua built a dam and grist mill on his fifty-acre "range" of land, marking the beginning of what would become West Epping village. The Folsom family owned several iterations of the operation, including a shingle-and-plaster mill, until the family sold the property in the 1940s.

Joshua was the first active Quaker in Epping, a heritage that Mary kept alive, though this presumably pacifist Quaker was also a patriotic member of the Daughters of the American Revolution. Joshua's son Thomas, Mary's grandfather, a farmer and miller, had a political streak, serving as an Epping selectman and New Hampshire state representative for eighteen years. Mary's maternal Bickford lineage also ran deep. Mary's application for membership in the Daughters of the American Revolution cites a Bickford ancestor, John Pease, who "gave material aid to the colonists during the war with Great Britain" and was "a member of Col Nicholas Gilman's Company raised to reinforce the Northern Continental army."

Though raised in Epping, Mary began her journals while living in Charlestown, N.H., along the Connecticut River, which forms New Hampshire's western border with Vermont. Mary lived with her sister Mabel, who had married the local postmaster, Fred Perry (the father of

Richard Hunt Perry, mentioned in the Introduction). Mabel, fourteen years older than Mary, taught in several schools and became a school principal in Charlestown. Mary's parents felt she would get a better education there than in Epping, especially with Mabel holding such an important position, Mr. Perry told me.

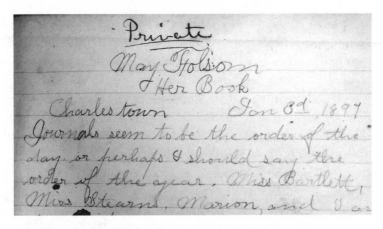

2. Mary's first journal entry, January 3, 1897.

Compared to the soul-searching passages that soon emerged, Mary's early entries were superficial, driven by events, not emotion. In this, Mary and I had something in common. I too kept a diary, beginning when I was ten. I maintained it for more than a decade and continued to keep occasional travel and other logs. Like teen-aged Mary, my young self took a mainly just-the-facts approach to journaling. Maybe I was afraid of prying eyes, something that also concerned but did not deter Mary. Truth be told, I lacked Mary's self-awareness, writing skills, and powers of observation. Much of my boyhood writing was instead pedestrian stuff and daily headline rewrites: Met Jeff and John after school. Went to student council meeting today. Boston Celtics won championship. Too cloudy to see total eclipse. I can't imagine that any current writer would be remotely interested in my journals, let alone one a century from now.

Mary was much more sophisticated and erudite than I ever was as she began her journal full of girlhood joy and innocence.

January 3, 1897
Subject. How I fell out of the Wagon.

In the afternoon I went down to the river again and skated for about an hour, but the ice was so soft that I soon had to leave . . . . Sophia Colton and Marion came along with the team and asked us to go to ride with them. So we rode down to the store watering trough and turned round. On the way back the girls pulled my hat pins out and first thing I realized my hat was in the middle of the road and I had the pleasure of jumping out and getting it. I thought I would not be bothered any more so I stood up in the back part of the wagon . . . . The horse was walking slowly and someone gave him a cut with the whip and first thing I knew I was sitting in the middle of the road.

Oh, how it did hurt! I thought for a minute I had driven my head off but after looking round I found I had only driven the head off of my hat pin. Today I feel as though I had been put in a mortar and pounded.

For Mary, Charlestown was far more interesting than her rural hometown one hundred miles away. Though both towns had populations of about 1,500 people in 1880, Epping was primarily a farming community, though its sizable clay reserves created a brick-making industry and its Lamprey River powered small mills, including the one owned by the Folsoms.

While Epping produced three New Hampshire governors during the 1800s, late nineteenth-century Charlestown was the most important legal center north of Boston. Settled as a frontier outpost, Charlestown grew into a place of culture and notable architecture (sixty-three buildings on the town's Main Street are on the National Register of Historic Places) and was home for many lawyers and judges. Nestled between hills and the Connecticut River, Charlestown attracted summer visitors to its large hotels. For Mary and her chums, that river was a wintertime expressway.

Jan. 17, 1897

Monday night we went on another skating trip. We went in three large teams and several small ones . . . . I did have a lovely

time all except one thing. The skating here is fine but today it
has snowed a little and I am afraid it is spoiled. If it would only
snow enough to be good sleighing I would not mind but to
have skating spoiled and no sleighing is enough to spoil the
temper of a Madonna.

Unlike the Mary who came to disdain formality, young Mary relished
proper social gatherings and was attuned to the fashions of the time, as
she noted after attending a ball back in Epping in an entry in which her
education, especially her appreciation of literature, was already apparent.

Feb. 22   West Epping
    I got home about two o'clock and thought that it would be
impossible to ever have so pleasant a time at a ball again. I felt
myself at that pitch of satisfaction in which one feels perfectly
satisfied with everything around them . . . . Two weeks later
came the Odd Fellows Ball. To my surprise I had a much better
time. At Mrs. Baldwin's Ball no one outside of this school wore
white dresses except Grace. At the Oddfellows', every one wore
light dresses, and in every way it was a more brilliant affair I
marched with one of the canton men and in quite a short time
every space on my ball-card was filled.
    Oh! What a lovely day it was. The sun was just rising as we came
out of the house and the air was full of frost which sparkled like
minute diamonds. The scene reminded me of a line from Scott.
"Each purple peak, each lofty spire/Was bathed in floods of living
fire." The snow was pink wherever it was touched by a ray and
taking it altogether was one of the most beautiful views I ever saw.

Not too far into her journaling, Mary needed to upgrade her pencil
hardware. "I find on looking back over your pages that I can hardly read
you in places you are so dim. If you don't do better I'll surely use ink. I
would anyway if I had a fountain pen of my own." Her brother Albert
gave her one a few months later. "I find a fountain pen very useful and it
doesn't seem now as though I could get along without one."

Six months after beginning to keep a journal, Mary had outlasted some of her peers.

> I wonder if any of the other four who started to keep journals at the beginning of the year have kept it up . . . . Whether Miss S still keeps hers or not, I do not know. Judging from appearances I should think her extremely apt "to change her mind," which is a "woman's privilege" as you know but perhaps as she has kept one before she may still keep up this one.

Mary began to worry about what to write down—and what not to. "I do not exchange many confidences this term. Now if I write much more I shall do as Fay does—point my finger at myself and say, 'Fool, fool, fool, hush, hush, shush,' for I'll say something I don't intend to."

Though spending time with her sister in Charlestown, Mary went to grade school in Epping and attended Sanborn Seminary in Kingston, N.H., a secular secondary boarding school that opened in 1883 a few miles from Epping. I grew up nearby and often drove past the big brick school building that was designed in the era's Victorian Gothic style. It was a far more imposing structure than the small wood-frame school Mary attended in West Epping. While an eager learner, her June 1898 Sanborn report card was mixed. Mary got mostly "A's" in English, history, and "Declamation" but fared less well in French and mathematics, getting a "D" for her one term of algebra and a "C" for bookkeeping.

Enter the Smiths

One Sanborn Seminary classmate merited special notice in Mary's journal: Maud Smith. "She is 'jolie et petit', and she was so nice the first day. Just see me use French, will you?" she wrote on November 23, 1897. Maud and her brother, Will Smith, become recurring characters in Mary's life.

While Mary's early entries continued to center on the daily doings of a young woman in the late nineteenth century, at times they reflected the broader world, notably looming war with Spain. Quakerism ran through Mary's bloodline, but pure pacifism apparently did not. Her reference to Congress still holds.

April 16, 1898

I wonder if I shall see war. I had thought that the greater powers were far enough into civilization not to have any more bloodshed, but the straws point for war. Spain and Uncle Samuel seem bent upon a quarrel. If the Maine, blown up in Havana Harbor the 15th of February, was destroyed by Spanish agents, with the knowledge of the Spanish government, <u>then</u> I hope that no American will rest until the loss of the Maine and her 238 men is avenged! But if such was <u>not</u> the case: if it was due to accident or to the work of private individuals then <u>surely</u>, thousands of women and children ought not to be made widows and orphans because two nations have a dispute. Congress is having a terrible time—fights with words and not far from fights with fists are the order of the day. Most of them are eager for war or at least for the recognition of Free Cuba. They don't have to fight.

Fitzhugh Lee is the hero of the day and well he deserves it. I am glad that he is a Democrat, for Democrats have good cause to be proud of him! "By Gory" when I get back to Kingston I'll make some such remark as that .... Won't they "hem" over it!

As consul general in Havana in 1898, Fitzhugh Lee, the nephew of Robert E. Lee and a Confederate Army general, was a strong backer of Cuban independence. Though he advised President William McKinley not to send a ship such as the *U.S.S. Maine* to Cuba, he supported the war after the *Maine's* sinking. He was offered a major general's commission in the volunteer forces set to invade the island, though the war ended before such an action was launched. Democrats backed such intervention on behalf of the rebels against the Spanish government. And the Folsoms were ardent Democrats. Not that they were gung-ho warriors. "My grandfather [Mary's father] didn't believe in fighting," Mr. Perry told me. "He paid someone to go fight for him in the Civil War."

Mary's awareness of Fitzhugh Lee and other current events reflected the rapid growth of news outlets in late nineteenth-century America. With the introduction of the Linotype machine in the United States in 1886, newspapers were able to boost their circulation. In an inverse of today's print news collapse, competitors clamored to join the inky fray. According to *Encyclopedia Britannica*, "The number of American newspaper titles more than doubled between 1880 and 1900, from 850 to nearly 2,000. In addition to the weekly newspaper serving the smaller community, every major city had its own daily newspaper, and the metropolis had become the site of circulation battles between several titles."

Items in the news became baked into school curricula. Mary and schoolmate Mildred Brown, whose daughter and granddaughter would end up owning Arcady, were supposed to be preparing for a debate about the merits of the Spanish-American War. Instead, they were lolling about "Hotel de Furbur," as Mary dubbed the eponymous boarding house that they shared while at Sanborn Seminary. Mary's April 16, 1898, entry continues.

It is so rainy today that Mildred and I are staying at home from school this forenoon and I thought I would take the opportunity to write a line or two in this. I started about nine and here it is after twelve and no farther along than this but Mildred and I have been talking so that explains matters. I am frightfully lazy I fear. Here I had six recitations this day and I only had four learned, and with all this forenoon to do it in I haven't touched the other two. Nor my debate either. You know, next Thursday night. The Polymian has a public meeting and Mildred and I have the sorrow of debating against Laburton and Bouvier on the question, Resolved, that the present war in Spain is justified on the part of the United States. We have the negative and of course we want to beat them tho we don't expect to.

Mary was likely referring to the Polymnian, a contemporary literary society. She and Mildred did not win that debate, but Mary had a deeper loss on her mind: the death of "Grandsire" Oliver H. Bickford, her mother's father.

Born in 1841, Oliver Bickford farmed in Epping and served as overseer of the town's poor farm. One of the few items I found in Mary's family home was a small, leather-bound notebook lodged under an attic floorboard. This was the "work book" in which Bickford recorded his purchases and sales, daily weather, and the status of hay and other crops, including corn, peas, and potatoes. July 2, 1859, was cold and rainy, he wrote, but "Corn from 6 to 12 inches hie." The next day, he "Begun haying." Bickford also listed local deaths (just the names) and occasional travels to Exeter and elsewhere.

The three-by-five inch work book was also his accounting ledger. On December 2, 1858, for example, Bickford bought cotton sheeting, a half dozen buttons, one ounce of thread, a half pound of snuff, one tin of tobacco, "1 Bush" of salt, one bar of soap and twelve feet of leather which, at $1.68, was his most expensive purchase of the day. All together, these items cost him $2.99, or about $95 in today's dollars. He recouped almost that amount when he sold fifty-nine pounds of cow hide to the Town of Epping for $3.24.

I could just imagine this well-worn work book resting snugly in the pocket of Mary's grandsire 160 years ago. Holding this small artifact in my hands made Mary's June 30, 1898, words about her grandfather feel much more personal.

> I do not know as I ought to feel as I do about his death but some how I can not regret it so very much. I loved him as much as anybody but I know that his faith encouraged him in the belief that he would meet all his loved ones again and I do not see anything to feel very sorry for, in that . . . . I don't think there is anything very bad in dying any way—only for those that don't. Those who are left behind are the ones who suffer. I am glad I am the granddaughter of such an honest upright man as Grandsire Bickford was. He never did a dishonorable thing and that is not the most common thing that might be said of him. I only hope that when I die I shall leave behind me a character as well thought of as his.

Mary used the occasion of her birthdays for self-examination. As she turned seventeen, she was already pondering her possibilities of marriage, a topic about which Mary would become much less light-hearted over time.

July 8, 1898

Since I began you Journal, I always intended to write in you on my birthday but somehow or other I never have succeeded in doing it until the day after . . . . Well, it is said that the third time never fails, so on my eighteenth birthday I will write in you if you and I are still in existence; and you shall have a description of May Folsom as she looks to herself. I only wish it could be as she looks to others for if "The gift, the giftie gie us, to see oursel as other see us, From manie a doubt and pain would free us." That isn't quite true to Bobbie Burns, but it means all the same thing.

I am seventeen! I am in my eighteenth year!! . . . . [N]ow I am as <u>old</u> as lots of girls who get married and go to keeping house. But I am not thinking of that possibility for not only is "Burkis not willin'" (provided she had a chance even) but I am sure "Willis would be barkin'" before the month was out if he only had cake, custard, and salads to live on. I am terribly deficient in such things as go to make up a good house keeper. I must learn to do better before July 8th 1899 for I shouldn't want you to be ashamed of your author, Friend Journal, and you will learn all about me then as far as I can tell you.

Mary was likely referencing Mr. Barkis (not "Burkis"), a character in Dickens's *David Copperfield*, who used that phrase to express interest in marriage.

Mary was not especially enthralled by her male contemporaries.

July 24, 1898

I have found out something new about boys. I never liked Burt and Bouvier very well for I thought their heads were very much swelled but I never did suppose that they were quite so silly. They had just been to a party the night before at which there were fifteen girls and only four boys. Perhaps <u>that</u> was something remarkable but there was no need of their making that the only topic of conversation and talking in the way they did too. If I thought that boys talked about me behind my back as they did about those girls I should want to go and live on a desert island where such a thing as "man" had never been heard of.

Despite her low regard for contemporary boys, Mary worried about them as the Spanish-American War ratcheted up patriotic fervor and military recruiting. This entry also mentioned schoolmate Maud Smith's brother Will, Mary's first crush, who lived in Raymond, N.H., which borders West Epping.

> July 25, 1898
> This morning I suppose Will Smith and the other Raymond men started for New York to take the physical examinations and if they pass they will enter the regular army for three years. I hope Will Smith will have some nice little ill about him that will prevent him from being accepted. Nothing bad you know—poor teeth—or something of that kind. Well I hope he will come out of it safe and sound and better for the experience he will have had. I thought this morning when I heard the down train go that perhaps that was the nearest I should ever come to seeing him again and it made me feel real sad for he is a good hearted boy in spite of other faults and I like him first rate.
>
> I don't see what boys like John and Will want to think of such a thing as enlisting for anyway. They're lots better off at home. Three years! I wonder what will happen in that time! He will most likely forget that such a person as May Folsom exists. I only hope Maudie won't for I should feel bad if that happened.

Will did not forget. A few months later, while apparently on furlough, he wrote to "My dear May" on November 20, 1898, to see if she could get permission "from Prof."—presumably a faculty chaperone or monitor—to attend a dance. "If you can I should be pleased to go with [you] if you so desire." Closing the letter by asking Mary to give "regards to your honeybunch of a roommate," he signed off, "From your friend William."

Mary did attend that ball, though Will was not her only focus. Rather, she wrote of "a little Nottingham fellow that was kind of cute and who I would like to get acquainted with." For a woman who in later years proudly declared herself a free-thinking Bohemian, young Mary felt strongly about proper social form, especially when it involved men.

West Epping, Nov. 27, 1898

I am awfully glad that I can do the round dances. It must be terribly stupid to have to sit out all the fancies . . . . I think it is lots more fun to dance with good dancers that you know than it is to run your chances on Tom, Dick and Harry. There is a place where I don't think "variety is the spice of life." I did two or three things that I never did before. My conscience reproaches me a little bit on that fellow that asked me to dance and I accepted and then danced it with some one else. I know it was a very rude unladylike thing to do, but if I had known when he asked me that I had never met him, also the condition that he was in, I shouldn't have dreamed of dancing with him. He was off in the first place to ask me when he had no introduction . . . . "Lady Washington" always was a favorite of mine, and Nichols is a dandy dancer. I am afraid it wasn't exactly proper for me to dance five times with him tho. But I guess it is all right for he is twenty-seven or eight anyway and I am only seventeen and altho he has got a big reputation of a flirt he only danced with me because we got along fairly well together.

This entry ended with more about the Smiths, with Mary worried about Will's health and Maud's silence.

Will is home on a furlough. He has been sick with typhoid malaria, and the poor boy has got an awful cough. He goes back the tenth of December if he doesn't get an extension of time. I think he is improved. He seems more manly. Dear me, I do believe the Fates are against Maud Smith's coming to see me. I've tried three times and failed every time.

A few months later, Will and Mary apparently defied the curfew set by boarding house proprietor Mrs. Furbur.

January 2, 1899

The Universalists had a fair the 1st of December [1898] . . . . Well, by ten o'clock when we boarding scholars have to go home the fun begins. It is awfully aggravating to see little kids in the Prep. class staying as late as they please, while I have to go home and just because they happen to live in town and I don't. Especially when I know my folks are willing that I should stay. I had an awfull hankering to stay to the dance two or three days beforehand. Then Will Smith asked me to go with him and then I was just bound to stay anyway for Mrs. Furber wouldn't have to look out for me and I wouldn't have wanted to make Will come home with me at ten o'clock. So I stayed. Right in the face of Providence or rather Prof. for he was there with his wife and daughters and sons. I felt terrible funny at first but that soon wore off and I did have a lovely time . . . . I told Prof. that I wished I hadn't and I did, but that isn't saying I am sorry. I had too good a time for that. James Beede is up here tonight playing chess with Albert. I am real glad it is Al instead of me that is getting beaten.

Two days later, Will Smith expressed remorse for his role in Mary's early rebellion. "I suppose you are home listening to a lecture from your mother about last Thursday night. I never will dare to go to your house now," he wrote. "This is the third time I have been the cause of your getting lectures. I hope old Prof won't be hard on you."

Will wrote about far less mundane events in an October 23, 1898, letter that offered a New Hampshire Yankee's searing account of the Deep South. Smith was stationed as an Army ambulance driver at Camp Wheeler in Huntsville, Ala., where soldiers were arriving to be treated for injuries and diseases such as malaria contracted during their service in Cuba in the just-completed Spanish-American War. Among the units recovering in Huntsville was the 10th Calvary, one of four Black regular Army regiments known as the Buffalo Soldiers. Members of the white 16th Calvary got into a skirmish with the Black soldiers almost as soon as the latter arrived in Huntsville on October 18, 1898.

Writing just days after that event, Will first expressed frustration with his fellow soldiers but then made clear just how little Black lives mattered.

Yes May I have seen a good deal of the South but I don't think I will ever ask Uncle Sam to pay my fare again if once I am out of this. About two thirds of the men every pay day get as full as they

can and of all the gambling one ever saw this beats them all . . . .
We are under orders to go to Cuba before the 20th of November. I
hope if we have got to go it will go then and we will get out of the
cold and then we get a 60-day furlough when we come back.

I suppose you have read an account of the 10th Cav colored and
the Provost guard [military police]. There were 11 men shot and
three killed. I was down to the depot and not fifty feet from the
fray in an ambulance. I tell you the bullets whizzed one went
straight through the Ambulance. So you see I have had the
chance to hear the bullets whistle if I did not go to Santiago.

We put the coons into the ambulance and brought them to
the hospital. One of them said to the driver that he was dieing.
The driver told him he could not help it and he died about five
minutes after. They all hate the coons here and no pity is shown
them no matter what is the trouble. They were to blame and
will all be killed if they don't behave themselves. Well I guess
I have told you enough of army life and won't cause you to
have the nightmares although I confess I had funny dreams
that night myself.

I was holding in my hand a first-hand account by the son of a New
Hampshire farmer of one of the many ignoble moments of American
racial history. I wondered if Will's Army experience contributed to his
alcoholism, which so troubled Mary and eventually was a factor in his
death. Today, Will Smith would likely be diagnosed with post-traumatic
stress disorder. He was discharged from the Army shortly before his
regiment was ordered to Manila for service in the Philippine-American
war that began in 1899. Five members of the 10th Calvary received the
Medal of Honor for their service in that war. And in 2009, a statue
honoring the Buffalo Soldiers was dedicated in Huntsville.

Back to the more local, the only significant development in Mary's
journal over the next few weeks was that she was to be a bridesmaid at
her sister Mabel's wedding. "I'll have to get Amy to tell me how to act
because of course she knows all about such things while I never saw a
wedding in my life," she wrote on August 21, 1898. "I 'spect' all we have
to do is to stand still and look 'pretty'." A July 24, 1902, letter to Mary

from schoolmate Mildred Brown began with her take on marriage and moved on to the bicycle as a new transportation option for women.

> It must be fun in getting things ready to be married but I am almost of the opinion that that is the extent of the fun. The more I see of young married couples the less desirable wedded bliss appears to me, though I dare say I am wrong. And so you enjoyed posing as a prospective bride. No doubt it is fun . . . . It is very quiet here and we don't dare to drive about at all for pleasure for fear of those dreadful automobiles. There have been several narrow escapes from accident about here. We do manage to get to the Post Office and get on the car but Mother and I do not dare to drive about as we used to . . . . Do you ride your wheel much this summer? Grace Knight and I are going to ride some afternoon soon.

The marriage of Mabel and Fred Perry produced two sons, including Mr. Perry, one of my Mary tour guides.

Chapter 2

"In my dreams the impossible is real."

Mary had "drifted apart" from some of her girlhood friends, but she remained concerned about one in particular—dear chum Maud Smith. Only after the fact did Mary learn of, as a local headline put it, "The Sudden Death of an Estimable Young Lady." The loss of her close friend triggered Mary's first devastating life turn.

> January 14, 1899
>
> Oh I have to write the saddest thing I've written yet. My dear little Maudie is dead. At three o'clock last Sunday morning she crossed to that unknown country "from whose bourne no traveler has returne" and Wednesday I looked on her dear face for the last time. Oh Maudie, as far as my human eyes can look, I can not see why you were taken . . . . If I could wish myself in your low bed if only you might be well and strong, but I dare not question the way of the Almighty, enough to fully wish it.

Maud died from typhoid pneumonia, Mary continued.

> She was delirious most of the time . . . . The minister prayed at her bedside a little before her death and when he rose from his knees she looked at him and said "I am going home" and she has.
>
> I have never lost so dear a one before. I loved my grandfather dearly, but it was different for I was prepared for his death and Maud's came so unexpected that I can't realize it yet. And he had lived beyond the threescore years and ten while she was nineteen in December.

For the first time in her journals, Mary raised the specter of connecting in the afterlife.

> Will sent a lock of her hair and I am very glad to have it for I have no picture of her. She was a dear, good girl, and would have made a noble woman. Oh, I pray that I may never do anything to

make me unworthy of her friendship . . . . Oh Maudie, come to me sometimes won't you. Come in my dreams for even that will help me—I wonder if those who are dead can return to their earthly homes in the spirit. If it is so I wish Maud would come back.

While her letters and journals made no specific references to her participation in the séances or the meetings with mediums that flourished during the nineteenth-century American Spiritualism movement, Mary was intrigued by the possibilities of the afterlife and parallel worlds. That spiritual hope helped Mary cope with Maud's death. Maud's family was also feeling extended grief, Maud's brother wrote on November 6, 1899, nearly a year after his sister's death. "Father will come home eat his supper and go to bed. Mother will cry half the time and I will go outdoors and smoke and go to bed. Father has not touched the organ once since poor little Maud use to play for he and I to sing." In the same letter, Will offered the first indication that Mary, who was in her final year at Sanborn Seminary, wanted to go to college. "You told me one time you had faint hopes of it."

Whether it was Maud's death or her own prospects, Mary was quite down on herself when the time came for her annual birthday entry, in which she cited the Mariana of a Tennyson poem. Mary didn't think she fit the era's standards for female success.

July 8, 1899

Eighteen! I May Folsom am no longer a child but a woman and oh, I am sadly fitted to take a woman's work in the world. I wish I were more competent but somehow or other all the talents have been withheld from me. To be sure I have a few brains I suppose but I don't know as they have served me very much yet.

Eighteen! and I am tired allready. Not all the time but very often I could say with Mariana "I am weary, weary, oh would that I were dead." Don't think I am unhappy or wicked 'cause I don't think I am either, but this last year I have been so tired of it all at times. I think I can dimly understand the longing of the Hindoo for Nirvana "the state of utter rest" with "passionless, motionless Buddha." That is not a high ideal, nor is it mine, but sometimes it seems a very comfortable ideal when one is tired.

Eighteen and truly I don't know much more than I did last year at this time except what I have learned in school and the fact that this world is full of gay deceivers and that I knew before. God grant that I deceive myself for that is better than to be deceived by others.

I promised to describe myself on this my eighteenth birthday, but I will save that until tomorrow. "The better the day, the better the deed."

"Tomorrow" indeed brought a more chipper mood. The second part of Mary's eighteenth birthday entry was among the most revelatory in the entire journal, even if Mary herself was somewhat dismissive. "I can tell you one thing, dear Journal, if a year ago I hadn't promised to write this description I shouldn't have been foolish enough to put all this nonsense down in black and white when I know better, but an out and out promise has to be kept."

Fortunately, Mary kept that promise. Her description of her eighteen-year-old self helped me to attach a physical presence and real personality to this woman about whom I had heard so much and whose words were before me.

July 9, 1899

Now to make you acquainted with Miss Folsom as she appears to herself. First for the outward description. I am five feet five inches tall and my average weight is 110 lbs. One time last winter I weighed 118 but usually 110 is a pretty good guess. You see by this that I am of the "lean and lank order." I am not at all graceful but I don't think on the other hand that I am conspicuously awkward. I have a very erect carriage and a peculiar gait. I don't know what it is but the girls all say they can tell me as far as they see me by the way I walk and Maud Smith said I walked as tho I had a broomstick down my back. Is that description sufficient? Mabel Reynolds says that my walk is different from most anybodys for I move only my legs. You know some folks walk all over but you might see me from my hips up and not know whether I was walking or rolling on wheels—so they say.

3. Young Mary in an undated portrait.

Mary next turned to her "inward description. There will be more truth than poetry."

> Away from home I have a real sweet temper. I hardly ever get mad altho when I do I never recover. But when I am at home right with my own folks I am ashamed to say that my temper flies

on the slightest provocation. I don't know why it is that I can't contend with those I love best in the whole world as well as with outsiders, but it seems I can't. Then too, I must confess I am lazy. If there never was such a thing as a book or paper I should be fairly smart but they have first place and everything else goes. As I have said before I have no talents. I can neither sing, play, or paint. I have some rhetorical talent but the necessary grace is lacking. I am quite fond of outdoor sports and can do most all of them a little but none excellently. The only thing that I excell in is English and history and there I am handicapped by not being able to pronounce the words I want to use.

What ever my feelings are I can think just what I please and my dreams of what have been, what might have been, and what will be or what may be I would not willingly exchange for anything else, for in my dreams the impossible is real and with out them I should have a pretty hard time. In some things I'd prefer the real article. For example with all my imagination. I have never imagined a kiss that I wouldn't exchange for the material one unless that one happened to be one of these little bird like affairs which you couldn't tell in the dark whether it was a touch of lips or a quick light blow of the hand. The dream is lots better than that.

It was getting too dark to write. "Perhaps this is the explanation of these last remarks for I think of such things in the dark more than I do in the daylight. I am eighteen! I hope I shall be a good girl this year. I am older than eighteen in some things, but in others I am terrible kiddish."

Perhaps exhausted by her birthday soul baring, Mary did not write in her journal again for six months. When she resumed, her entries became centered less on daily activities and more on her moods and her observations of the people and world around her. So while a July 6, 1899, letter to Mary from a Sanborn Seminary schoolmate named Ethel referred to Mary having "a great time at Dartmouth" College, where Mary's brother Albert was a student, Mary made no mention of such a visit in the journal. While peers wrote mainly of the mundane ("I am going to have me a hat pin made out of an army button that I was given once," wrote one. "This button has been to 'Cuba' too."), Mary explored far deeper thoughts. And she still despaired over the death of Maud.

> December 31, 1899
> "The old year's dying in the night. Ring out wild bells and let him die." Oh may the unseen hand wipe out from my heart all impure thoughts with this old year's passing. I have struggled with them but they are still there and God alone can drive them out. If He does not do it what can I do? But I believe He will . . . . The clock strikes—1,2,3,4,5,6,7,8,9,10,11,12. Happy New Year Mary Evelyn. Poor little dear, the new year I mean, not Mary Evelyn. He won't get his little feet cold on the snow tonight for there is no snow to get them cold on. I wonder if he has had his youthful innocence chilled and frozen by "sights and sounds unholy." I wonder if he has had his youthful ideals smashed already. It will come. Good night, my journal. School tomorrow.

Mary feared that Maud's brother Will was in a downward spiral, driven by drink.

> Jan 8, 1900
> True were the words of David that the years pass like a dream that is told. A year ago today I was wishing and praying and hoping that Maud was better and would get well. And at the very time she was already cold and dead and I didn't know. And now the year is come again and altho the pain is not as sharp I think sometimes it is harder to bear . . . .
> I know that her brother my friend would not be entirely a joy and delight to her if she saw him—unless indeed her vision is more perfect than ours. But I condemn him not for he is hers and besides am I sinless that I should throw a stone? I have thought thoughts that are not speakable and I have said words that I ought not and I have done deeds that I am ashamed of. And truly I meant to be good and I do now as far as that goes, but Oh dear how little things are.

Like many a teenager, Mary was impatient with local and family constraints on what she could and could not do. She still planned to go to college, based on a July 30, 1900, letter from a school mate. "I see by the paper that you have been admitted to College," it read. "I am glad for you. Hope you will succeed." A letter from another classmate similarly asked, "Are you still planning to go to Plymouth?"

The reference was to the Plymouth Normal School in New Hampshire. Beginning with the opening of the first one in Vermont in 1823 and the first state-funded one in Lexington, Mass., in 1839, Normal Schools, so-called because they sought to establish the norm for teacher training, spread across the nation, opening higher education doors to women. By the early 20th century, the moniker was dropped in favor of "teachers college" or something similar.

But one or both of Mary's parents scuttled her plans to attend college, probably due to financial woes of the small family farm and mill operation. Mary was crushed. And she felt trapped in her small rural town.

> 14 July 1900 West Epping, N.H.
>
> Since I last wrote in you I have graduated from Sanborn Seminary and . . . I have also finished my hopes of a college education. I think little and say less for it would make me more discontented with my lot than I am. I would be content if I only had a little freedom—if mother would only realize that I am not a free careless girl of five but that I am old enough to take a little care on my shoulders. She does not think I can do anything—which is very true and what is worse she will not let me try. I feel as tho I wasn't one bit of use—only a piece of expense. She cannot know how humiliated I feel. It is something to have to give up hopes of a college education or of teaching school making myself independent. West Epping is an awful place. Not one single companion of my own age in it. Nothing but low gossip, vulgar talk and oaths. None of these do I wish any commerce with. There is quite a contrast between what I wanted and what is within my reach. I'll stop talking this stuff.

4. Mary's Sanborn Seminary graduation photograph, 1900.

For all her gloom, Mary had a good time at her graduation, based on this July 14, 1900, letter from Sanborn Seminary roommate Edith Hilliard, who threw a dig about Mary's fondness for Will Smith.

> May my dear. Uh, My, did you have a fine time at commencement? Did you have a <u>fine</u> time in the hammock! Uh, May I thought the hammock wasn't big enough for two, but I guess two can manage to get in once in a while can't they? You got in to ride with Will Smith "so as to make it easier for the horse" you must have had quite a load.

Social graces still mattered to Mary, whose July 14 entry continued with a description of a gathering she hosted where one friend "seemed to be having a wretched time."

I was sorry to think my guest should not enjoy herself. I wonder when it is proper to be unpleasant. The hostess must be hospitable and entertaining to her guest, the guest should be ready to fall in with the plans of the hostess. There certainly can be nothing unpleasant between those two, and as for being disagreeable to ones fellow guest—that, I speak from experience, makes the hostess uncomfortable. It seems to me the only chance to 'have it out' is to stand on the street corners and 'jaw' and that is unladylike. I think every thing that might hurt another's feelings is unladylike.

Mary pondered that term. "What a lot of meaning there is in our old Saxon words . . . . 'Lady' 'woman' 'man' demand so much from us if we only lived up to them. If we did, the Golden Age would come again and the angels would visit the children of men. We should see them and talk with them with our bodily senses as well as our spiritual ones."

Mary was crossing the bridge from adolescence to adulthood. "So you are nineteen years old and have a bicycle," wrote schoolmate Emily Tapley on July 25, 1900. "I hope you are not weighed down by the grave responsibility of the former fact nor worn out by the use of the latter article."

By the 1890s, the redesign of the bicycle from one marked by a gigantic front wheel to something like today's version made bicycles all the rage, especially among women. "Bicycles extended women's mobility outside the home," according to the May 17, 2018, *Smithsonian Insider*. "A woman didn't need a horse to come and go as she pleased, whether to work outside the home or participate in social causes. Those who had been confined by Victorian standards for behavior and attire could break conventions and get out of the house . . . . The bicycle craze boosted the 'rational clothing' movement, which encouraged women to do away with long, cumbersome skirts and bulky undergarments."

Mary embraced the bicycle rage, which ended with the arrival of the automobile. A mutual friend spoke of "riding by your house and of seeing you mount your wheel," Edith Hilliard wrote on July 3, 1900. "I am so glad you have one, because you spoke of wanting one so many times. I hope you will enjoy it very much." A week later, Edith wrote that she was feeling "lots better" after an illness. "Mama keeps fussing about my going to the doctor, which I don't think there is any need of."

Edith was fatally mistaken. "Edith's last letter," Mary penciled onto that letter's envelope. The death of a second girlhood chum rekindled the despair Mary felt over the death of Maud Smith.

> 21 July 1900
> These pages will soon become only the record of sorrow. Another dear friend has joined the "great majority." My dear little golden haired roommate Edith Hilliard bade farewell to the world last Tuesday the seventeenth of July. She was eighteen the day before I think. Our ranks are broken our union shall never be complete until we meet in the grand reunion. I shall miss my dear little girl sadly. I did not expect to see her for sometime but I little thought we had said our last farewells.

A July 27, 1900, letter to Mary from Edith's sister Mary Hilliard detailed what happened. Edith had been tired, the sister wrote said, but she resisted seeing a doctor.

> Edith . . . wanted to live to be an old woman and be able to say that she had never had any need of a physician . . . . The next morning her breathing seemed to trouble her and we had the Dr. come as soon as possible. Shortly after he came she became delirious and in a few hours she went to sleep. At three o'clock I woke her to give her some medicine and then she went into a stupor from which she never awoke and passed away very easily at last, her breath growing shorter and shorter . . . We cannot quite understand why one so young and who was just beginning life should be taken but we feel the Divine Power orders everything for the best.

Mary Folsom shared her despair with a former teacher, Jeanette Moulton. In her July 22, 1900, reply, "Miss Moulton," a Wellesley College graduate from nearby Hampton Falls, addressed Mary's loss of both her young mates and her college hopes.

I can't answer your question why such lovely girls as your two friends are taken away either but I know that the people we seem to need and love most do go. I often wonder if it is because they do not need the discipline of life longer . . . . I am disappointed that you cannot go to college. [A friend] says probably you are one of the girls who do not need to go to college to learn how to live. She says that some of us are poor stupids who have to go to college to get the ideas put into us while other girls—like you, I think—can think most of these things out for themselves.

In a Christmas Eve day, 1900, letter from Brunswick, Maine, schoolmate Elizabeth Worthley also sought to console Mary about missing out on college. "It is a grand privilege of mine to be able to go [to college] and I don't appreciate it fully I know, but it reminds me of something John Cram said once, 'We do not realize the pleasures we enjoy until it is too late, and then they come before us like haunting spirits.'" Perhaps to further soften Mary's disappointment, Worthley detailed her weekly schedule, including, "Saturday mornings I clean up faculty rooms to bring in a little penny."

Longer gaps opened in Mary's self-described "unperfect chronicle." But her cleverness occasionally returned, as when she anticipated the gender pronoun challenges that would face writers more than a century later as she made passing reference to that year's severe flu ("the grip") epidemic.

17 January 1901

We have met the grip and we are his-hers-its. We are "thons." Once some wise people thought they would get a word meaning masculine or feminine gender, singular or plural number, so they mixed up our "they" with the French "on" and got "thon" out of it. Some how it isn't used much in common everyday speech. I am sure the grip is masculine, feminine, singular, plural and common to all creatures here below. Edith came down with it first then Mother and then Ed. Papa and I haven't "succumbed" yet, but there is time.

Mary chastised herself over her writing inconsistency. "Now why don't I write oftener?" she wrote on June 23, 1901. "When I become some famous authoress as foretold by my friends, doubtless this journal will be very valuable."

For now, Mary was less worried about fame than her immediate future. She had begun her teaching career at the age of nineteen. Her lack of a college education did not prohibit her from entering that profession. Though Normal Schools offered more advanced training, teachers in rural towns such as Epping often had little or no post-secondary education. Well into the early twentieth century, these teachers taught basic reading, writing, and arithmetic and some geography and history to as many as eight grades combined in one or two-room school houses such as the one that Mary attended and later oversaw.

Beginning before the Civil War, teaching became increasingly female, and by 1900, women, many of them Normal School graduates, comprised more than 70 percent of American teachers (superintendents and principals remained mostly male and were better paid). Though wages were low, teaching was a source of income, independence, and purpose for women. Mary noted that she was now a teacher just a year after graduating Sanborn Seminary.

> June 23, 1901
>
> This spring I have taught my first term of school. Whether I've made a success or not remains to be seen but I think I have done fairly well. I've had eighteen scholars from the first to the eighth grade. They are trying to grade the schools this year so that makes it harder. Also it is the school where I used to go myself and the four largest pupils I have been to school with.
>
> A week ago Friday I went to Kingston to the Commencement exercises [at Sanborn Seminary] . . . . I saw most of the girls and boys. Oh dear me "the little rift within the lute" of class harmony has begun. In some cases it is anything but small. I think the gulf that grows between friends is an abyss indeed. I think I prefer to think of Maud and Edith as they are rather than to have had them live and grow little.

Mary's casual use of lines such as "rift within the lute" again revealed her erudition. The phrase, based on a work by poet Alfred Tennyson, refers to early evidence of disharmony among people who had been close. In an entry a year later, Mary, prompted by something she said or did, displayed her own internal disharmony.

> July 31, 1902
>
> Oh Mary Evelyn when you <u>know</u> why, oh why, don't you live up to what you know. There is an excuse for those who are ignorant altho if they sin they needs must pay some penalty . . . . How much greater must the penalty be for those who know and yet deliberately fall short of their ideal? To be sure, what I am reproaching myself for is something nine persons out of ten wouldn't give a second thought to. Is my conscience too tender or what is the trouble? . . . . The punishment usually is in my own mind. My self-respect goes round clothed in sackcloth and ashes and wailing "Lost, lost, lost."
>
> After two or three sleepless nights spent in contemplating this uncanny visitor I begin to feel better and vow that I will never do that thing again . . . . Perhaps you think that I harp more than is needful on that word "self-respect." Truly it must not grow to self-conceit. But if I, knowing my own temperament, making all excuses for myself yet cannot respect myself, how can I expect anyone else to be kinder to me than I am to myself. "Ay, there's the rub." Truly "The mind is its own place and of itself can make a heaven or hell, a hell of heaven."

The entry continued with Mary returning to her curiosity about spiritualism.

> Had I lived in the old days I should have wanted to be an Epicurean in prosperity, a Stoic in adversity. Perhaps I did live then. "These shadowy recollections" may come down from some free far off life when the world was new and men had no guide save their own will and the pleasure of the minute. It seems sometimes as tho a little door in my brain blew open and for a

second I lived the life of other days. Sometimes I do something, a little simple thing perhaps, and I know that I am repeating something done before. I meet a stranger. His face is familiar and some chord is awakened which has slept perhaps since Remus leaped the mudwalls of Rome. Who knows? Wisdom is a realization of how little one knows. Now that sounds like an epigram but as far as I know I never saw it before.

Mary dreaded that the next nine months in her classroom would leave her "in purgatory," as she wrote on August 20, 1902. She was glad that her deceased chums did not have to face the world in which women such as Mary had to live. "The older I grow the more thankful I am that [they] haven't got to go thru the pain and sorrow this old world holds for a woman."

During my travels, I found relatively few letters written by Mary. I especially wish I had the one that she wrote to former teacher Miss Moulton in which she must have offered some blunt views about teaching as well as relationships with men. Based on this return letter from Miss Moulton, Mary was not feeling especially positive about either.

August 9, 1903

I was interested in your certainty that no man existed without whom you could not survive, but that some books must be finished. One of the Kingston things that I always remember about you was going to bed late after dropping your book on the sticky fly paper. I am expecting that a man will arrive for you at any minute and you will give up your "heresy" without a gasp . . . .

I am sure from your letter that you think you do not like teaching school. I am sorry that you feel so about it for it is pleasant in some of its aspects. [But] I wish my young class occasionally heard what I say to them. Last year I had a room of forty two juniors to care for with twice as many boys as girls. They were the toughest boys in school but I am rather fond of that kind so we got on all right. Next year I am to have all boys the first day I shall be frightened to death.

   Mary, who liked to write poetry, ended the first book of her journals with verses, mostly mournful ones about loss, including this one about an afterlife in which she would reunite with Maud and Edith.

> As the dry earth longs for the rain
> I long for thy face again
> If the life I have to live
> Were mine, I would freely give
> If giving would bring thee to me.
>
> Still in my heart I know
> By the sun's bright glow
> By the starry splendor of night
> By all things good and right
> By the flower in the grass at my feet
> That some where we must meet.
>   Or all is not complete.

Chapter 3

"They haven't beaten Mary Evelyn yet."

Mary began the third book of her journals with a quote (slightly altered) from Anglican clergyman and writer Charles Kingsley.

> Be not anxious about tomorrow
> do today's duty: fight today's
> temptations: and do not weaken and
> distract yourself by looking forward
> to things you cannot see.

That somber preamble matched the mood of an older (though still only 21), more pensive Mary who was pondering her career choices.

> August 24, 1902
> When I commenced the other book I was a little school girl in Charlestown. Now I am teaching school myself. How little do we see into the future. I will prophecy that five years from now I shall have tried nursing and if I am not a success at that I shall be teaching somewhere. I think I shall be better content with what ever I may be doing than I am at present for I shall be twenty-six and probably possess the "philosophic mind." I am sure I hope it will be a better mind than it is at present.

"At present" Mary was miserable in West Epping. Her family had deep ties to the town's schools—before moving to Charlestown, Mary's sister taught in Epping and her brother was on the school committee—but Mary came to detest teaching in the town, based on a May 7, 1902, letter from Rachel Stannard, a Sanborn Seminary classmate who was teaching in Lawrence, Mass. "You poor child," Rachel wrote. "After you have labored so hard with those unpromising scions of West Epping youth, I think it is too bad if you have had persecution and criticism from those who could not do half as well themselves and don't know beans about the work. I don't doubt that you have done splendidly with the school."

Maybe, but Mary was anxious to be done with West Epping. "My school is well nigh five weeks gone," she wrote on October 9, 1902. "That is a cause for rejoicing for after five comes six and then it is half gone." Several months later, as Mary again sought refuge in her journal she also worried about people discovering what she wrote.

> March 16, 1903
> My dear Journal. My pen is a stranger to your pages, yet many times my mind has confided in your wisdom and I have seen, in fancy, all my trials and tribulations set down in your pages. That is a wise way to do for it saves time and keeps me true to my creed of not putting down in black and white anything that can do anyone harm or that I do not wish to have known. Still it is a very unsatisfactory way and after all everyone in this family knows that I do not wish anyone to read this book. If they, knowing this, disobey my wish, they ought not to kick if they find something that doesn't please them. It is the principle of "Listeners hear no good of themselves." In case of my death I shall try to provide that they don't fall into anyone's hands that I don't wish them to.

If Mary left instructions about what to do with her journals and other material, they were either lost or neglected. I recognize the ethical quandary about publishing words that their writer intended to be private, but I've convinced myself that Mary's writing deserves to be shared, a view supported by her closest relatives as well as former students and others. We all wanted others to be able to appreciate Mary's writing, such as her rat-a-tat-tat verbal snapshots.

> March 16, 1903
> I've made a number of new acquaintances lately. Charlie Leddy—Blue eyes—long nose, hooked, short upper lip, rather humorous expression to his mouth which also shows—unless I'm way off in character reading—that he isn't made of ice and snow. firm chin enough good forehead, rather jerky in his movements. Has sense and looks very trustworthy from a woman's point of view. Not very handsome but I like him. Twenty four. Ralph

Goodrich, one of a pair of twins—nice kid . . . about seventeen or eighteen. He will be an awful flirt if he keeps on for he can't hardly keep from hugging all the girls now. Uneasy as a fish out of water. I like him too. Grace Knight . . . comes from Hampton Falls and teaches school at East Epping. She has hazel eyes and a very nervous disposition. Interested in the affairs of her friends. I like her. Stewart Mallard. Recently joined the eastern star. Stooping shoulders, Van Dyke beard. Macchiavelli! Dr. Butterfield. His eyelashes are very light. I can't stand light eyelashes.

Other new people merited more extensive descriptions, including a Dartmouth classmate of her brother Albert "who will succeed in this world. The manner in which he smokes and eats convinces me of that. Take a six foot man, a three inch pipe, an unlimited supply of fine cut in a bead embroidered bag and the air of a Diogenes—there you have Dr. Herbert Augustus White . . . It is great fun to watch any one that has that philosophical calm."

Despair continued to lurk behind the lightheartedness of such snippets. Besides unhappiness with her job, Mary felt tension from the house next door, where her brother Edwin and his family lived. The Folsom family mill, which Edwin operated, was facing financial woes.

March 27, 1903
I shall be glad when a year from now comes and I can look back on the events of the next few months as a part of my past, something dead and done away with and forgotten, as I can forget those things that trouble me when time has thrown his shadow over them. With poverty, failure, and debt staring those I care for in the face, to say nothing of the general atmosphere of distrust and deceit and mutual dislike hanging over these two houses it is enough to drive one crazy. I don't care much about the school. It is kind of aggravating but they haven't beaten Mary Evelyn yet.

"I'm afraid that last sentence was rather blind," Mary wrote about two weeks later. In one of this journal's longest entries, she was bitter about complaints lodged against her during her first two years of teaching in

Epping. In her telling, some people just didn't understand her classroom ways, such as allowing her students to burn off energy outside, which some parents felt was proof that Mary permitted an unruly classroom.

The attacks on her, Mary suggested, were really aimed at her father and brother, who had accused the father of one of her students of stealing wood. She was confident that she was in the right and school officials approved of her classroom work and manner, but she was hurt that "this canaille have spit their spite out on you." (Mary's vocabulary again being superior to mine, I had to look up that synonym for rabble.).

Mary felt trapped. She was twenty-two and had a respectable job, yet people challenged her classroom ways. She was still living at home, with parents who had cut off her hopes for college. Friends, she feared, would think her a failure.

> 17th April 1903
>
> I haven't said much about my school for it is such a thoroly disagreeable subject that I don't like to write about it. The first term I taught wasn't very bad. I think I may say I liked it. The next fall term was fairly pleasant, but the winter term was the most unpleasant that I have ever taught. It was the first term that there has been a winter school here and the children didn't like to come and there was no good opportunity for them to get much out of door exercise. Things went hard. I lost my grip and got completely discouraged. It didn't seem as tho I could teach another term, but mother was very anxious that I should and so I taught again last spring and last fall. I think I may say that I got my grip back again. I didn't have a bit of trouble.

Mary continued to keep "a much better school" but then the daughter of the alleged wood thief began to act up and things became "very wrathy."

> Immediately a spirit of insubordination appeared. If I told the children not to roll in the snow next day it would be "My folks are willing that I should roll in the snow" etc etc . . . . Everything I asked of the children was done in a very disagreeable manner.
>
> Still, with all this, my order in the school room this winter was

35

better than last winter . . . . During noons and recesses I
encouraged their playing in the schoolhouse, for many days they
couldn't get outdoors and I wanted them to have some active
exercise. Of course they made a great deal of noise. I may have
made a mistake but it was done because I wanted them to, not
because I wasn't able to help myself.

Mr. Hulse, Epping's school superintendent, supported Mary but
some disgruntled Eppingites wanted her gone.

[W]hat should they do this spring vacation but go round with a
petition asking for a change of teachers on the grounds that I was
"utterly incapable of keeping order." And such yarns! I had let
them run over the desks and jump out of the windows in school
was their principal one . . . . I dare say that when I have been
home at noon they have run over the desks and jumped out of
the window but it seems to me very unfair and unjust that things
should be told as taking place in school which have happened
when I was half a mile away from the building.

What especially irked Mary was that none of the petitioners had
children in her classroom. None had even visited it, she wrote. Still, they
"wanted people to go to school meeting to vote for someone 'to turn
May Folsom out.' Everyone who has been in school refused to sign it."
When the school board met, Superintendent Hulse said it "would be a
great injustice" for Mary not to keep her school.

[He said] I had done good work and brought it up. He said he
should never know it to be the same school that he first visited
two years ago. My children read the best of any in town and
he didn't know but what they read better than in any other
school he was ever in, and I had done good work in other studies
considering the material I had.

Mary switched to a different school in Epping. She remained bitter about the complaints against her but she was going to show that she was in charge of her new classroom.

It was pretty hard the first day but I strapped one small boy in the afternoon and managed to convey to the children's minds that I wouldn't put up with such nonsense. The strain is considerable for I feel as tho I must watch them every minute. I shall be thankful when the next ten weeks are done. Then, not even to spite my enemies will I ever step foot in that building as teacher again.

It makes me angriest to think that the ones I have tried hardest to help and make something of are the ones who have tried hardest to hurt me . . . . "The mills of the Gods grind slowly" but I have seen them grind pretty small. If this is a punishment for some wrong of mine I am glad to face it now instead of hereafter. I will confess to you, journal, what I have scarcely owned to myself, that this is pretty hard . . . . I think how my friends will talk it over and think there can't be quite so much smoke without some fire and pity me and think I'm a failure and don't amount to much. That cuts dreadfully . . . . I can't relish the prospects of those who are not my own people thinking I am a failure when I'm not.

Continuing this entry, Mary feared the loss of her fledgling career and the little independence it provided. "A year from now I shall probably be at home for we shall have six cows then and mother won't be able to do the work. The work must be done by somebody and I am afraid I am the somebody. Well, I like a farm."

Mary fancied herself prescient about the future, but her cow-milking vision would prove just as wrong as her pledge to never again teach in Epping.

"I am half afraid to take the lid off and look within."

Another young death shattered Mary when her older sister, Mabel Folsom Perry, died on January 1, 1904, three weeks shy of her thirty-seventh birthday. The cause was "septice" following three weeks of pneumonia, according to the death certificate, which listed Mabel as a "housewife," though she had been an educator. "When I taught [in Epping] I simply worshipped her—years have not taken away from the feeling," said one of the many condolence letters to Mary. Mabel, wrote another acquaintance, "had the dignity and earnestness of a woman even while enjoying herself as a girl."

Mabel's death triggered the same despair and questioning of faith Mary felt after the deaths of girlhood friends Maud Smith and Edith Hilliard. "I have always been able to have such faith for other people in their grief and now when it has come to myself faith has taken wings," Mary wrote on April 20, 1904, her first entry since Mabel's death. Despondent and self-doubting, Mary was glad that her late sister did not know "what a poor, weak, flighty thing is the sister of whom she was so proud. Does she wonder as I do why that sister should have been left and she taken?"

> I know this much. I would have gone in her place. I know it. I know it: and it is written "Greater love hath no man than to give his life to his friend." I would have done it, oh so gladly. Will it be remembered for me at the judgment that twice in my life I have loved well enough for that, and this last time I would have held it as a joy. Oh, I feel so little and poor and weak. I do the things I know are wrong. I'm not fit for everything. I have felt that I didn't care, that every evil thought was welcome. I would follow the passion or impulse of the moment regardless where it leads me. If the strong are taken and the weak left, what else can God expect of his world?

Her sister's death, Mary continued, had undermined her faith and moral center.

> These temptations that assail me no one knows unless the ones who have passed beyond, and perhaps they may pity a little tho I deserve it not . . . . I have never given way to my lower nature as I have since she has gone. All my temptations and tribulations come from my own self. They are from within. That makes it worse. Sometimes temptations come from without and for the love we bear the tempters we commit great crimes and burden our souls with sin. Love for others covers a multitude of sins . . . .

I would never think of stealing a man's money but sometimes I find myself slurring his reputation. I might love a man with every fiber of my being thrilled to his touch but if he sought me otherwise than honorably it would be in vain: and yet there are thoughts come to me that are more degrading than any act of mine could be and when I think them I feel as tho she knows.

Mary's religious faith wavered.

Oh, God, if your thought is for any of us, if you care, help me to help myself. I would not have said "if" once, but when your own Son said, "Ask and it shall be given" and I asked so hard for one thing and you give it not you made me feel as tho there must be an "if" somewheres. And what I asked for was only the life of a woman, the mother of little children . . . . I only asked that the living might not die. I asked and you did not give. Was it because the asking must be of things spiritual only? . . . . Help me. Help me to keep from evil [thoughts]. And this above all. Make me worthy of being her sister. Don't make her ashamed of me. I ask this and if it is not granted, thy Son spoke words of false hope. That can not be, can it?

In a short entry a few months later on August 15, 1904, Mary paraphrased a parable. "The past is a memory, the future a dream: only the Present is real: only the Present is thine. Live then in the present."

Chapter 4

"I'll try to be strong for myself."

Mary left her journal untended for a year, not returning to it until August 25, 1905. "I have thought that I would give you up but after all it is pleasant to have some record of things that have past and when I read over the pages that I have already written I wish that I had made a completer record of the past two years." Though happier in her new job at the Red Oak Hill School in Epping, Mary was still uncertain that teaching was right for her. "Everyone of my children seemed to like me and when school closed in the spring they all urged me to come back. They were kindness itself but the school was small and I felt as tho I didn't care for it. In fact I thought I didn't want to teach any more anyway."

After two years at Red Oak Hill, she took a job in nearby Stratham, N.H. "Everything has gone beautifully this year and I expect to go back in the fall," she wrote. Mary had another death to mourn, "my dear Ma Smith," the mother of Maud and Will. Mary was worried about Will.

> [Mrs. Smith] died of a horrible lingering disease—cancer— from which she had suffered for more than two years but the end was very peaceful in her old home in the very room where she was born. I hope she and Maud are happy together. They said her last words gasped out as the breath left her body were "Tell - Will - to - be - a - good - boy." I hope sometime he will be what she wished.

Living away from the West Epping Quaker Meeting, Mary attended various Protestant churches. The subject of one Sunday sermon in Stratham was, "What must I do to be saved." Among the minister's "guideposts for salvation," Mary wrote on November 15, 1905, was "service."

> He said if we tried faithfully and honestly to serve others the rest of the things would come to us. I didn't believe or rather agree with all he said, but it made me feel as tho the little things didn't amount to much after all. The little things have been

amounting to considerable lately and I wish I had had sense enough not to let them take up so much of my time, thoughts and conversation, especially my conversation! And yet today I am troubled by a "little thing." Mr. Morrison superintendent of public schools dropped in on me this afternoon and the floor was awful dirty. I can't get it out of my mind.

Mary shifted quickly from ambivalence to wit and insight when she next picked up her fountain pen.

March 4, 1905
The spirit moves me to write this afternoon and yet I know I shan't really write the things I would like to and most likely I shall write the things I could well leave unwritten.

I always feel like saying "May blessings be upon the head of him who first invented weather as a subject of conversation." I think that when Adam awoke from that certain deep sleep which we have all heard of, with a sore feeling in his side which tradition has handed down to us as caused by a missing rib, but which may have been heart trouble or too much green fruit—I say I believe Adam's first remark most have been "It's remarkable weather, Eve." Well this is remarkable weather.

Mary went on to describe the dating "game" of her day, adding a clever recitation of her moment with "A-."

Heigh-ho! this game! Sometimes I think it is going to be too much for me this time. Last summer I felt a little worried for fear my partner—I mean my opponent—it hasn't got to partnership—might burn his fingers, but I reckon he can take care of himself. Trouble is there is a chance for a threecornered game and I know if I get into that it will be my own fingers that will get burned. I avoided some burnt fingers last summer pretty well. Really it was awfully funny—the game is worth it after all . . . .

Then there was the evening when "A- and I were alone in the tent."

> Now A- is a wee bit, well affectionate—he's all right tho— I'd
> been thinking something might happen if I didn't watch out and
> I thought the "something" was mighty near. A- was anyway. He
> seemed afraid my hands were going to be cold. Now I don't mind
> a man's being "near" if there are plenty round and surely keeping
> one's hands warm isn't a "seen," but when he gets "near" when
> I'm all alone with him, especially if I don't dislike him I begin
> to feel all kind of wobbly and not in the right state of mind to
> properly "sit" on those little demonstrations of affection which
> convention doesn't approve of, but which apparently the "natural
> man" does, most highly.
> Well, I must confess I felt "wobbly" but I couldn't very well tell
> him not to do it—because he wasn't doing it. I just had a feeling
> that he would in about two minutes and that without my lief.
> Suddenly something inspirational came to me. I put on the most
> languishing, affectionate, dreamy look I could muster up and I says
> in tones of longing "<u>Do</u> you suppose Billy will come on that train?
> Ah, I <u>hope</u> so!" A- flops over on the other side of the couch in high
> disgust "Don't know! Hope so I'm sure" and he didn't seem to
> have much appetite for any further affectionate demonstrations.
> Now I'm wondering if he thinks other folks have better luck.
> Well they don't, anyway not yet.

Mary's journals captured moments of daily life, such as "an interesting adventure" on March 11, 1906, when she "went over to the creamery with Laura Willey. Horse scared at a load of grain, jumped, broke wiffle tree and crossbar, ran, pulled Laura out over the dasher, lipped me out into the mud. Didn't hurt either of us and didn't spill the cream! We were very lucky."

5. Undated portrait.

A few days later, Mary mixed in a bit of politics.

> Tuesday was town meeting day. The Democrats defeated the
> Union ticket, much to the surprise of the Unionists who weren't
> looking for it. Yesterday Edith and I had an oiling bee and oiled
> the dining-room floor. She tells me that Rachel Stannard has been
> sick with diptheria. It seems to be quite prevalent this winter . . . .
> I hope mother isn't going to be sick.

On April 1, 1906, Mary recorded impressions of more new
acquaintances, including a woman in whom Mary perhaps saw
something of herself. "Decision—firmness—a will which shines out
thru every feature until when I look at her I see—almost—yes—quite
an embodied will and intellect—almost as tho the flesh had dropped
away and instead of a skeleton one saw—well intellect. Some what self
centered inasmuch as she is apt to consider the outcomes of anything
entirely from her point of view."

"Does that Bohemia exist except in imagination?"

The 1906 school year over, Mary was back in West Epping, worried
about her brother Edwin's struggling mill operation on the Lamprey
River, though she did not want her concern to show, as she wrote on
June 30, 1906. "No outsider shall have a chance to console or condole.
I'll try to be strong for myself and those I love too."

About a month later, Mary was recovering from side effects of a
vaccination required by her school. "I suppose it was a good thing but
like many other good things it was mighty well disguised," she wrote on
August 2, 1906. I had a similar reaction to my Covid-19 vaccine shots
nearly 115 years later.

Mary continued this entry with one about a Fourth of July picnic in
Stratham that "might have been better" were it not for "the everlasting
and unnecessary fuss the folks make about my going near the water."

> I'm foolish to let one of these "little things" stir me up so but oh
> no one knows how happy it makes me to be on the water. I love
> it. And I'm twenty five years old and not a fool and I don't go

unless it is safe. They wouldn't say a word about my riding or going in an auto and there are just as many accidents in those ways as there are on the water, but I suppose they think it is more comfortable getting ones ribs stove in or your neck broken than is an involuntary bath or drowning.

The irony was that in later decades, Mary taught her students and others how to swim at Arcady. Even as she neared the age of eighty, Mary swam alone to a small island a half-mile out in the lake. Those early admonitions about water risks may have been triggered by a boat trip Mary took to Appledore Island at the Isles of Shoals, a sparkling archipelago of nine islands about six miles off the Maine and New Hampshire coasts. Mary described the cottage of poet Celia Thaxter (1835-1894) about eight years before fire destroyed it in 1914.

August 6, 1906
It was a beautiful, soft, hazy day with the water so still and calm that a canoe might have gone safely. Oh for a canoe on some vast water way! We went into the cottage into a room lined with beautiful engravings with many vases of flowers standing about. Most of them were of plain clear glass with only a flower or two in a vase—the little flowers in the little vases and the large flowers in the large vases. But I like best the impression as I stepped into the room, which curiously enough is one of out doors. A long long dark walled room with a wide window at the end looking out on the sea. The land sloping abruptly enough so that nothing of it was seen. My eye was held by the shimmering changing gleam of the sea, a symphony in blues, soft, varying from the light misty blue to the dark purple that marked the faint line of Hampton shore and beyond that the sky like another sea, greater, illimitable . . . so vast, so near, so far, so all around, that it seemed as tho I gazed down a vista of eternity—for it was without end and without beginning.

Mary's description "certainly rings true of other descriptions of the parlor and magic of the place," Jennifer Seavey, director of the Shoals Marine Laboratory on Appledore Island, emailed me. Thaxter died in 1894, Seavey noted, so by the time of Mary's visit "someone was keeping up the parlor and Celia's tradition regarding flower arranging. The hotel was waning at this point . . . . I bet it felt a bit more mysterious as a result."

Perhaps suffering the same writer's block that I've often faced, Mary left another long gap in her journal. "Gracious! It <u>has</u> taken a year to recover from that," she wrote as she resumed her entries on July 15, 1907. "Now this year . . . I'm going to try to write an account of special days that strike me as being worth it. Days to be remembered—oh they are many this past year if I had only kept account."

Mary was now teaching in Foxboro, Mass., where she had more new acquaintances to describe, including her "boarding mistress," who was . . .

> . . . married to a man several years her senior, a born coquette of the harmless kind because she is too kindhearted to do much hurting unless she has a special grudge against someone. Very, very kind to those she likes, temper of a Tartar. I think she likes a social life to cover up memories of more joyful days. She knows this world and the inhabitants thereof and I like to sit and see her pull the little strings that cause puppets to dance her way—she is a master hand. When it happens to be my string that's pulled it isn't quite such fun, but I like her because she has lots of grit and much of good with a nice little spice 'a la diable' to make her interesting.

Another new person intrigued Mary.

> Ruby Sloan—oh Ruby Sloan. I'd like to know if those inscrutable eyes of yours haven't seen a few things and if those red lips of yours couldn't tell a few things. You are quiet—mighty quiet—but it is the quiet of knowing not of ignorance. Perhaps I'll know you better a year from now, but if I do there will be things you will be silent as the Sphinx about. You're the kind that tells not all she knows. And you are wise not to.

If Mary did get to know Ruby better, she did not tell her journal about it.

Mary recognized, with some satisfaction, how her "days to be remembered" could clash with prevailing norms. Freed from her classroom, she was able to pursue more special times, such as a nighttime sail on the Great Bay, a tidal estuary on the New Hampshire coast. "It was full moon and the breeze was just light enough to fill the sail and no more," she wrote on August 6, 1907. "The boat drifted so still and silently down thru the water with its white sail glistening in the moon light. It was so beautiful with something of the unearthly about it. The silence, the moon light, the wide calm bay, that towering white sail—I shall never forget it."

Mary's spirits were buoyed by her summer sanctuary at Arcady, which was built one year earlier in 1906. (See Chapter 12.). The bungalow offered safe harbor from the churning undercurrents of Mary's life. Nestled in the natural world she craved, Mary could literally and figuratively let down her hair. By the lake, Mary enjoyed time with the people to whom she was the closest. And her fascination with mythology and spirituality could flourish, as she continued this entry with a reference-filled description of an "Enchanted Isle far from the sight of men."

It always has blue skies above it, sparkling water around it and a little breeze talking thru its pines. In that island-locked cove nymphs still play in the waters drying their white bodies in the wind and the sun. It is a place for lotus eating—for dreaming— for living a quiet day—perhaps for loving a little while life is young and the warm blood of youth flows red in one's veins.

Lucky thing I've such an imagination. Other folks would see a rocky little knoll with a few scrubby trees on it, but for me it is the Enchanted Isle. It is a type of something that lives within me, of a quiet, happy, simple and natural plane in my life that I wish there were more of. So for us all life has its Enchanted Isle and we were better did we visit there more frequently to gain strength from its strength, peace from its peace, rest from its rest.

Too often, we store away and forget our own Enchanted Isles "in some far corner of our hearts," the entry continued.

> And with it are happy days of childhood when fairies and gnomes and nixis held sway. When we built our fairy boats and made our fairy courts with green moss thrones and gray moss couches all ready for the fairy queen. When we put our lips against some gray rock, muttering mythic spells, hoping and half believing that the rock would roll away and show us the entrance to the treasure world down below. When real and vivid walked thru our daily play the characters who long ago have played their part and gone forever to their Enchanted Isles. And things always came out right. Mary's fair head never rolled from the scaffold. Lady Jane Grey and her lover husband lived to a ripe old age. Jean D'Arc closed her days at Domremy and told us stirring tales of how she escaped the English, led by her Blessed Voices. Wallace was always rescued.
>
> Forgotten too, the quickened heart beat at the sound of the Hermit thrushes clear tinkling note as it peals out when the sun throws the long shadows eastward. Forgotten—all forgotten, except for those who keep their Enchanted Isle ever fresh, and visit it often in memory's boat. If the song says true, "The world is no place for a dreamer of dreams," and so 'tis no place for me it seems. Aurevoir.

Mary followed this long passage with one on September 15, 1907, that was as intriguing as it was brief. "Oh what a bother are garments of gladness. No getting near to good old mother Earth and feeling her great heart throb with yours. Because, frail mortal, 'you'll soil your dress'— Burr!" We don't know what social or other restraint so irritated Mary that day but her delight in the freedom and camaraderie of her "little side trips to Bohemia" continued to ring out.

> November 2, 1907
> I'll write in you twice this month. 'Twill take all that to tell about the mad merry doings of these last six weeks. 'Tis the weekends

that are mad. They have been little side trips into Bohemia. Oh Bohemia—you're such a fascinating little place with your unconventional doings, your lights and laughter and tinkling glasses, your dishes spiced with strange variety, your women, your men who wait not for an introduction but raise their glasses and drink to us "not only with their eyes" as we pass by.

Care, dull care, is well hidden away, but oh, I wonder. Bohemia should be a place where fellow holds out a hand to fellow— comrade meets comrade—democracy should reign supreme and every one's motto is "What I have I give thee" of good will, of mirth, of help, joy, experience, tales of strange countries—all that goes to make life happy. There should be no regard of sex, or beauty or wealth—just comradeship, a drawing together of mutual tastes. Does that Bohemia exist except in imagination?

Mary's use of the phrase "dull care" was likely intentional. During their annual secret encampment, members of the Bohemian Club, a San Francisco men's club founded in 1872 by a group of artists, intellectuals, writers, and others, began performing a "Cremation of Care" ritual to liberate club members from the "dull cares" caused by work, finances, and other sources of stress.

Mary often referred to Bohemia. A poem in one of her journals, for example, included a poem that she titled, "In Contrast—Bohemia," with this last stanza:

> Who would not seek Bohemia
> And all its carefree crowd
> Who would not seek that happy state
> To laugh a while at humbled hate
> That e'er by Mirth is cowed.

Bohemian Mary still clung to certain social standards, however. On December 1, 1907, she wrote about having friends over after her dramatic "debut" as Eliza Briggs, a character in "A Rival by Request," a comedy in three acts written in about 1896 by Benjamin Lease Crozer Griffith, whose work was a staple of amateur productions. As

she compared herself to the character she played, Mary opined about
"affectionate demonstrations."

> [Eliza] is a very forward, slightly overdressed young damsel,
> something of a flirt and coquette. Very foreign to my nature, I'm
> sure. Only trouble is I've studied being Eliza lots more carefully
> than I've ever studied being myself, and it would be shocking if I
> found myself being more Eliza than Mary Evelyn!
>
> Oh, I spoke of the night after, didn't I? . . . . You know, journal,
> my sentiments about affectionate demonstrations. I do if you
> don't. Well, it is just hard work when two are demonstrating, and
> the third is willing for the fourth to live true to her ideals. Human
> nature is human nature. What a pity the Lord didn't make me
> a little bit superhuman! I wanted to be human . . . . It is late and
> I'm weary. Fare well journal.

Part Two

Searching for Love

Chapter 5

While young and more carefree May Folsom wrote mostly of outings, dances, and other social events with male and female chums, a more serious writer soon emerged as Mary pondered romance and marriage. She grew more somber as contemporaries married and had children. While wary of "playing partners," she showed interest, to varying degrees and at varying times, in two men. The first was Will Smith, the older brother of her dearly departed girlhood friend Maud Smith. Mary's second male interest was Ralph Gowen, whom Mary met when she was in her twenties.

She ended up with neither. Not until she was thirty-five did she find a man to marry in Edmond Blair. And that was only after her deep relationships with two women. Not that Mary didn't draw other romantic interest, some of it unsolicited. "I know I am asking a great deal of you, but I do hope that I may be the favored one," wrote one determined suitor in 1913. Mary copied her terse response on the back of the letter's envelope. "Sincerely hope you will find the happiness you are seeking, and doubtless desire, but which it is quite impossible for me to bestow." She added a penciled note to herself. "Would have been more sympathetic if I hadn't happened to have seen the predecessor of this note a year ago, same words underlined."

Gentlemen suitors

Will Smith first appears in Mary's journal in 1898 when the two are teenagers getting into occasional curfew or other trouble. Things between the two might have developed further and faster were it not for Will's decision to enlist in the Army in the run-up to the Spanish-American War. By the time Will returned to New Hampshire after his Army stint, another man, Ralph Gowen, was getting notice from Mary

Gowen, who was born about a year earlier than Mary, studied engineering and was in a military program at New Hampshire College in Durham, later the University of New Hampshire. Mary, who was twenty-four and teaching in Stratham, left the romance door open after spending some time with him.

April 1, 1906

All I can remember is the difficulty he had unpinning that cloak I had on the night I joined the grange. Then the night I told his fortune in the canoe. I told him he had a strong will-power and was very persistant and there was only one girl that he would ever love and he'd finally win her. I told him true as to the persistancy but if the "one girl" is the one he seems to have chosen for the present I doubt if the rest comes true. However it may. I can tell better two or three years from now. He's a good honest fellow, trustworthy.

Gowen referenced that same floating fortune telling in a letter to Mary two weeks later. "My horoscope has come from the astrologer in Bridgeport. It is a pretty good one, almost as good as the fortune you told in the canoe down on the Bay."

Based on Gowen's letters—Mary's journals made little mention of their outings together—the two enjoyed skating and other activities. Always the teacher, Mary also sought to give an intellectual upgrade to Gowen, who dutifully reported that he was reading the books she recommended, including one he "liked very much," perhaps because of the protagonist's romantic success. "The hero showed plainly that he believed in the adage that faint heart never won fair lady, though the obstacles were many," Gowen wrote on November 14, 1905. "He got the girl and was happy as of course it should be."

Gowen was uncertain about Mary's level of interest in him. "This letter is as much about me as any I have ever written," he wrote on January 31, 1906. "But I hope that, on that account, you won't be so disgusted with it and me as not to answer this letter of your friend . . . Ralph E. Gowen".

Mutual acquaintances noticed that the two were spending a lot of time together. On March 7, 1906, Gowen wrote that he had a light course load that semester. "I shall be able to give some grounds to some of the rumors that have been floating around even for the one that asked whether I was stopping in Stratham and only visiting here [at school]. I thought that that was putting it rather strong enough."

Gowen was likely the potential "partner" about whom Mary wrote while she was back in West Epping after the school year ended in Stratham.

June 30, 1906

"Home again, home again." I do believe those words are the best music in the world. They ought to be the climax of some great triumphal march to be sung by every home returning child. But then what's the odds? They are sung in our hearts and sometimes the silent music is the best of all for it accords with God and nature.

That little game I've been telling about has been quite brisk this spring. I'm rather inclined to think we may play partners sometime. He would have had it so already but I'm not sure as he knows his own mind so we'll continue to be opponents for two years more. Incidentally I may find out my own mind by then and that's no small problem. "First I would and then I wouldn't . . . ." Anyway, if two years are as long as the last two weeks have been, I'll be seventy-five and gray-headed by then. Two years are an <u>awful</u> long time, don't you think so journal?

That reminds me that I am well nigh twenty-five and honest I do begin to feel old-old-old.

Two years passed and Mary marked the end of her relationship with Gowen.

August 28, 1908

Since January—since last August in fact—but more since January, I have done a lot of thinking and I had come to the conclusion that I could never be more to him than I am or have been. So he came and I had to tell him so and he was so good and so unselfish with his "Don't worry about me; it is your own happiness that you must see to," that I, who seldom weep, cried half the night and wished with my whole heart that I could find him another girl, so much better than I, so much more lovable, that he would think me a dream and thank God from the bottom of his heart that the reality was better than the dream. Will he ever?

I hope so. But I can never never find him myself. I kept the letter of my promise at least. I waited two years and no other man had any chance during that time—and there were one or two "might-have-beens."

Perhaps the Lord will put that much down on my side. So that game is finished. What would you call it—a draw, my game or his? Mine, for I have not surrendered. His, for he hasn't either. A draw is best.

In an entry she labeled, in all capital letters, THE BLUES, Mary also dismissed any marital possibilities with Will Smith ("Billy").

January 19, 1908
It is such a luxury. I've got the blues journal, actually allowing myself the privilege of the blues, and what is more I'm going to set 'em all down so I can see them all and laugh about them afterward and then not be foolish again. It will be such a fine lesson for me when I feel real chipper again. Now let's have the two underlying causes. Firstly, it's Billy. Secondly, in order to forget firstly I've been going it so much that I am just tired to death and molehills look like mountains.

I think Billy and I are thru. I really don't care so very much but after all, when you have been letting one man take up most of your thoughts for about two years, even tho there is a large "if" in the way, it leaves sort of an aching void when you decide that the "if" is a certainty. Lesson No. 1: Never let one man monopolize your meditation for any length of time again. There is safety in numbers.

The "if" that deterred her from Will Smith was probably his drinking problem. Both men—and the possibilities lost—remained in Mary's thoughts. She referenced a tear drop-shaped blob of ink on a journal page as she wrote of her fading interest in Will and Gowen—and men in general.

November 2, 1910
I had a letter from Ralph Gowen a way off in Argentina not

long ago . . . . Somehow or rather my experience with him has
taken my desire for other men away. No that isn't it either. It is
more like this. I find myself comparing other men with him and
they don't shine. There was an innate decency about Billy that
was rather taking—and I'll admit he came nearer to being my
master than any other. Gee! It isn't everybody can shed such an
inky tear as that in memory of an old lover. I couldn't if I'd had
my pen screwed up.

By then, Gowen was in Buenos Aires working at "Oricini
Meteorologica," according to the October 1909 *New Hampshire College
Monthly*. He went on to serve as an infantry corporal in France during
World War I and eventually became a turbine tester for General Electric
in Lynn, Mass., where the 1940 U.S. Census reported him living with
his wife and two children. He died in Exeter, N.H., in 1967 at the age of
eighty-seven. Will Smith spent the remainder of his life in his home town
of Raymond, where he was a cutter in a shoe shop. He was just forty-
six when he died in 1924 from leukemia, with "chronic alcoholism" a
"contributing cause," according to his death certificate.

Even before Smith and Gowen, Mary fretted that being tied to any
man could cost her the freedom and intellectual independence she
cherished.

> October 27, 1911
> "[T]here must be three elements in perfect love. A man
> must be able to make you respect him, he must be master of the
> situation—and—he must be able to arouse that emotion called
> by so many different names—love, lust, passion, desire, or what
> you will. I've wondered if there are more things necessary. One
> must respect the father of her children—or ought to. You'd like
> to have a man that you'd never feel ashamed of—and surely the
> Hunger is not implanted in the marrow of our bones and fostered
> in our blood never to have it feed on its natural food. Starvation
> is hard.
>
> I've seen lots of men that I've respected, many that I've
> admired, a few that have answered the third requirement but
> really—the combination is hard to find. Burr! Me and Diogenes.

57

A few months earlier, Mary mocked the motivations of some of the men she met. Yet she was also jealous, even resentful, that other women, including some with whom she grew up, found husbands in such men and had children, while she had neither.

> April 22, 1911
> It is awful when you realize that the only thing an unmarried man likes you for is because he likes the good feeds you give him, or because you have such charming girl friends that their presence gives him pleasure. And the married men like you because you can listen intelligently to their conversation and ask them sensible questions to keep them wound up on. This being a disgruntled old maid is not all it's cracked up to be. Never mind, cheer up, Mary Evelyn. It's not half so bad as it will be ten years from now.
> There's Ida Ross sitting over there rocking her baby. She's nineteen and I'm twenty-nine. I suppose she is fulfilling "woman's highest destiny." Does she realize the grandeur of motherhood any better than I could. Yet it is her kind that finds its mate and become the mothers of the race, and it is my kind who—don't.

A visit that summer to a Shaker village in Enfield, N.H., prompted further pondering of romance and passion. Mary was intrigued by the Shakers, who called themselves The United Society of Believers in Christ's Second Appearing (the term "Shakers" derived from the group's energetic dancing.). Mary's Quaker upbringing would have drawn her to the Shaker belief in gender, race, and economic equality. Mary was also intrigued by Spiritualism, which "was of great interest to the Shakers and many went to presentations about the topic," according to the Shaker Heritage Society. Spiritualism—the belief that the living can communicate with the dead through people with special powers known as mediums—was popular in late nineteenth century America, including in New Hampshire until the movement faded in the early 1900s.

The Shakers' approach to male and female contact and relationships interested Mary as she described her visit to Enfield on August 3, 1911.

Only a half century earlier, the village was home to about 300 Shakers, she wrote.

> Now a scant fifty hold sway over the big barns and the Great House. This morning [we] found one of their graveyards, the quaint little stones, all alike, with their names, the dates of their deaths, and their ages, nothing more. Yet I found them fertile field for my imagination. A few died young but most of them were well on in their 80s and 90s. I wonder if they lived so long because the fires of their passion never flamed up but smothered under a wet blanket of repression until smothered in their own ashes. Did they find peace and rest, surcease of woe and worry in their green fields and orchards, in the constant round of seed time and harvest? Was their fraternal and sisterly affection sure anchorage for their human hearts?

Mary was ambivalent about the Shakers' efforts to dampen "sparks" between men and women.

> There's the quaint old mounting stone, built for the sisters to step into the old high chaise without need of a brothers helping hand. There is also a caution in their rules against a brother and sisters conversing in a room with closed doors unless another brother or sister is present. They were pretty careful of sparks. I have been interested in their reasons for leading the celibate life. It is very similar to the doctrine advocated by the modern Esoterics and various other psychical societies who hold that the highest life can be lived only by the virgin in body—those set aside from the flesh—of the spirit only. It seems at odds with the eternal madonna-worship of the long ages past. Were they wrong?

Maybe Mary was still having such thoughts about two months later as she recounted a visit from Gowen. Three years after opting out of a relationship with him, Mary concluded that her former suitor was probably better off "in the arms of Louie," a presumably more compliant partner. (Gowen married Myra Edith Hutchins, a school teacher, in 1919.). For her part, Mary bemoaned her spinsterhood.

> October 27, 1911
>
> I don't know whether [Gowen] liked his entertainment or not. I've never heard. Probably not. And I don't know whether he liked his entertainer or not. Probably not. Probably he is seeking pleasant thrills in the arms of Louie. She'd make him a good wife. Giving all he asked, when he asked, ruling his home in a nice, precise, old maidish way, looking up to him as a superior sort of being, gossiping and back-biting with her neighbors in her accustomed way. Burr! I guess maybe they'd fit well. Heigh-ho! He and I wouldn't. When I got to giving, I'd be too very generous and then I'd dream dreams and see visions and while I'd own him Lord and Master sometimes, I'd have my turn in leading. That wouldn't suit him. Well, I don't need to moralize. Such things will no trouble the head of Mary Folsom—spinster that was, and is, and ever more shall be!

Chapter 6

"One girl's treachery"

While the end of things with Gowen and Smith saddened Mary, it may have made her more open to finding comfort with women, including two to whom she became especially close. The first was Marian Snyder. The second, and much more significant, partner was Anne Reed. From roughly 1908 to 1914, Mary described numerous "days to be remembered" with the two, many of them at Arcady where, in a sad twist, Marian and Anne each met the men for whom they left Mary.

Mary's connection to these women was certainly emotional and spiritual, if not more. Mary and Marian and later Mary and Anne supported one another and regularly stated their love for each other. Such open expressions of love and devotion to other women were common at the time, in part because men too often offered neither. "In nineteenth century America close bonds between women were essential both as an outlet for the individual female's sensibility and as a crucial prop for women's work toward social and personal betterment in man's sullied and insensitive world," historian Lillian Faderman writes in *Surpassing the Love of Men* (1981). Mary's journals and letters confirmed Faderman's statement that the "expression of those feelings was often committed to paper."

Faderman, an internationally known scholar of lesbian history and literature, adds that until the twentieth century, "The sexual potential of love between decent, healthy women was still unacknowledged by many seemingly sophisticated authors; sound women were asexual." Citing the words of a nineteenth-century British judge in a case involving charges of lesbianism against the co-founders of a British girls' school, Faderman writes, "It was doubtful enough that [women] would concern themselves with any form of sexual satisfaction, but that they would seek sexual expression without a male initiator was as credible as claiming to hear the thunder play 'God Save the King.'"

Faderman cautions against viewing nineteenth-century female relationships through a contemporary lens.

> Perhaps love between women was permitted to flourish unchecked in the nineteenth century because the fact of the New Woman and her revolutionary potential for forming a permanent bond with another woman had not yet been widely impressed upon the popular imagination, as after World War I when New Women emerged in great numbers. It was then that love between women came to be generally feared . . . . The emotional and sensual exchanges between women, which correspondence and fiction tell us were a common form of affectional expression for centuries, suddenly took on the character of perversion.

Another of Faderman's books, *To Believe in Women* (1999), focuses on middle class, professional women who were in intimate relationships with other women in the late nineteenth and early twentieth centuries. "I use the term 'lesbian' as an adjective that describes intense woman-to-woman relating and commitment," Faderman writes. "The individuals [in this book] might all be said to have had 'gender trouble,' in the sense that they could not accept the restrictions inherent in the notion of gender: they were dissatisfied with the way the category 'woman' was constructed, and they were frustrated by the limitations placed on them as forced members of that category."

Those words certainly applied to Mary and Anne, though the precise nature of their bonds remains uncertain and largely irrelevant. Mary herself hinted at conflicted feelings about intimacy. "Why am I made the way I am?" she wrote in 1913. And in a letter, she thanked Anne for sending a photograph that Mary would "look at it when I get the blues or feel 'degenerate' for it will remind me that there are some mighty good things in the world." Even after Anne's engagement, Mary wrote to her that "No one can ever take thy place, dear heart . . . . There will never be anyone else . . . . Isn't there a little spot in the hollow of my shoulder where only thy dear head fits well? And isn't there a large spot in the hollow of my heart where only thy dear self fits well?"

"Our mutual teasings"

Marian L. Snyder was born in Northford, Conn., in 1887 and taught with Mary in Foxboro, Mass. She soon became Mary's colleague and kindred spirit.

> July 15, 1907
> Daughter of a Congregational minister—brought up in fear of the Lord and therefore with a very strong bias towards the devil and his works. A strong fighter, a good hater, a faithful friend, and a defender of those who speak not for themselves. Some time more trouble than she is yet aware of will come her way, perhaps brought on by her own impulsiveness, perhaps by someone's untrustworthiness. It's due to her love of the unconventional that there have been so many days to be remembered for I too love the unconventional, and "what people say" troubles me not. She leads where I like to follow—sometimes to tell the truth, where I'd rather not.

Mary's next passage refers to Italian Renaissance author Giovanni Boccaccio, who wrote the *Decameron*, a collection of novellas, in the aftermath of the plague outbreak in Florence in 1348; Filomena (correct spelling) was the narrator. The entry resonated during our own pandemic more than a century later.

> There were those days when the diptheria scare held reign over us and Marian Snyder and I held <u>rein</u> over it. We drove too, it didn't drive us, glory be! There comes back to me a vision of our rattling over limerick writing our epitaphs, discussing sociology, doing everything except worry. It was fun and we needed the rest. But still if it had been diptheria, it would have been a pretty serious affair and I can understand the feeling that drove the cholera victims to their ill-timed mirth and dancing, or Filomina and her followers to the walled in palace courts where they indulged in the naughty tales of the Decameron. Naughty but instructive!

Perhaps some sort of triangle was forming among Mary, Marian, and a friend named Rob, whom Mary first referred to as "Marian's boy." Mary, who for some reason was convinced that the shape of peoples' mouths defined their personality, was uncertain about Rob "for there are lines about his mouth that tell a story and a world wisdom in his eye that confirms it. And then I doubted if he had any great respect for women until he had proved them worthy of his respect."

> July 15, 1907
>
> I used to think he came <u>some</u> for love of Marian and very much for love of Robert Dow. And thinking that he didn't see Marian in quite the right light I was afraid of him—for her. She never would be for herself. And so I used to lie awake nights listening for his footstep on the stair and drawing a sigh of relief when I heard it. But either I misjudged him, or he changed, or he is one of those who when they find a woman is all right have nothing but respect for her. This spring when the "man" appeared on the scene and insisted on the dismissal of the "boy" I found myself taking up arms in defence of the latter much to my own surprise.
>
> I'll bet one month's salary if she had stayed there another year "propinquity" would have had another marriage to its credit. Darn propinquity!

Marian became an Arcady regular, though her Connecticut upbringing was apparently much more refined than life at the rustic bungalow.

> August 6, 1907
>
> All the days at Pawtuckaway were worth remembering and many of the nights. The first night when I got so beautifully warped sleeping in the hammock. The night that Marian Snyder came. Poor child, she came from very civilized civilization. I had fears that she might not like the lapse to barbarism but she stood it. But that first night when the whip poor wills kept up their mournful call all night, and two or three dozen big bull frogs in the cove under our window incessantly shouted for their "jug-a-

rum, jug-o-rum" and the mosquitoes buzzed over our heads with occasional painful nips, and the bed—husks on slats!—Poor Marian! It is small wonder that she rose at three and sought rest on the cove. I heard the rattle of oars in the oar lock and slipping my kimona on over my night-gown I hastened after. I found her clad in her bathing suit which went very nicely with my kimona and thus arrayed we sallied forth on plunder bent.

The nature of "the plunder" was unclear; blueberries or blackberries are a good guess. In a letter, Marian wrote that she looked forward to more special days together.

> April 8, 1908
> It was a fine visit I had with you, dear, one of the right kind. Perhaps our mutual teasings, for I insist they are <u>mutual</u> help us to appreciate more the moments when we use each others' brains. I hanker for you and the bungalow. Be sure to save (us) some days for us two alone. They are the days that stand by us that keep us in tune. You don't jangle out of tune as I do and for that reason you are an example to me.
> I love you
> Marian

Marian restated her feelings for "Mate Dear" Mary a few weeks later. "How busy the times are now with the Memorial Day preparations and the final celebrations ahead. Won't it be heavenly bliss to have it all over. It is doubly good to see ahead no separation between thee and me. We can live lives alone and independent, but how much more we can be if some one who loves you has recently been near." But just months earlier, Mary had confided to her journal that she suspected something was going on between Rob and Marian.

> January 19, 1908
> I had looked forward to seeing them . . . and thought how nice it would be to have 'em "luf" me some and "smove" me ruffled feelings even tho they didn't know they were doing it. You

see I was hungry for a little petting and affection to sort of fill
up that void. Well, during the week I had been skating with Rob
who had been very nice about taking me, bless his heart. Some of
Marian's last year kids knew about it and thought it was terrible
mean of him to take another girl. It was a huge joke to me and I
thought of how Marian would appreciate it and laugh too. Well
with her usual ability to do the unexpected, she pretended to sail
into me in great shape for flirting with her property, and it was so
totally different from what I looked for that instead of its seeming
funny, it hurt.

Mary veered into self-pity about "growing yellow." She'd hoped her
close female friends would offer solace.

I'd asked a fellow here to be nice to [one of Mary's female
friends] and he was so darned nice that it was a little more than
I bargained for. Second Fiddle is all right but it is wearin' some
when you ain't first with anyone. Especially when you've just
finished being first and no one has applied for the vacancy and
you're twenty-nine and growing yellow and it seems to you that
your girlfriends don't love you as much as they do some other
fellow and nobody loves you—Boohoo. Ugh! You ain't beautiful,
and you ain't interesting and you just ain't nothing but a little
foolish, insignificant never has been and never will be. Oh, it's a
slick little feeling. It is good for you tho. I realize it after a night's
sleep, but it hurt yesterday when I was selfish and tired and self-
concentrated enough to wish the girls to think of me and love me
sort of audible like so as to heal my wounded pride.

One day, Mary appeared unannounced at Arcady and Rob and
Marian seemed surprised rather than pleased. Marian noticed her
disappointment, Mary wrote. "She caught on to something wrong and
if I had had time to tell her would have soothed me into an amiable state,
certain. I'm mostly amiable just to think of her. I do love her."
Marian sought to further to smooth things out in a letter a few
months later.

June 2, 1908

The outdoor air and wetness have proved very invigorating, after all. I feel as fresh and ready as if I had been sleeping long and hard. I knocked a youngster over with one hand this morning. Don't you pity Rob?

In spite of your disgust, well merited disgust, my joking about that subject keeps it from becoming tender and embarrassing to us, so please let me continue to beg your congratulations.

The last good time was a dandy. It seems as if each one were better than the one before. Do you ever feel that way? It's a "beauchiful feeling . . . . The rain pattering on the water as you and I came in impressed me and so did another thing—it was "How different the <u>tone</u> of our bungalow is going to be." Yet there will be just as much and more fun in it.

Marian ended her letter with a telling limerick.

I love you both
I couldn't help it if I would
I wouldn't help it if I could.

"My faith in one girl had rather a heavy jar."

Rob wasn't the only man Marian met at Arcady. Mary noted other visitors, including one named Osgood who "has had an unfortunate love affair, too." As a result, "he has analyzed himself so minutely that he hasn't a proper conceit of himself" and was constantly distracted. Mary quite approved of Osgood.

August 6, 1908

The Fourth marks the beginning of the two most interesting weeks in one way. 'Entrez les hommes' in the shape of ye men from Manchester. first Stearns, Osgood and Hamlin, later Nightingale whose name is the translation of something unpronounceable in Jewish, and who is one of the dearest, gentlest souls. When he unmercifully beat me at chess it was done in such an apologetic way that I was charmed . . . .

[Osgood] is a lawyer, a lover of lakes and rivers. 'Earth and her waters and the still depths of air.' a student of Omar and Spencer and Ingersol, fond of the dance, of chess, of argument <u>and</u> a Sunday school superintendent! Contradictory, isn't it? He believes that ones chief pursuit on this earth is happiness but, he adds, the highest happiness is right doing. I sincerely hope he'll never find that happiness is gained by doing other than right. I don't know what he measures his ideas of right by for he seems to have discarded the usual standards—love or fear of God, hope of reward, or fear of punishment, believe in the hereafter, etc, and has set up some standards of his own. It must be a good one for he is one of the decentest, cleanest men I've ever had the good fortune to meet.

Mary was attracted to Osgood, at least intellectually. As she came to understand that he and Marian were becoming involved, Mary was less upset by their blooming romance than by what she saw as their keeping her in the dark and taking advantage of Arcady to advance it. Mary was angry as she turned to her journal on a rainy day in Foxboro.

December 7, 1908
My little world has upset itself topsy-turvy and I've had hard work to readjust myself. I feel as tho the guide ropes that have always held me secure to my ideals of love and friendship and sincerity had loosened and left me adrift on a sea of uncertainty— all because my faith in one girl had rather a heavy jar.

A little thing to make one doubtful of the truth of all, is it not? It won't always. It is getting better. But sometimes I feel in despair of ever feeling again the utter, complete unquestioned belief in the sincerity and loyalty professed by others. I doubt it in myself. And a belief in the unchangeable loyalty of good comrades has always been the dearest belief to me.

I've let this affair with Marian make too big an ache. It has made me morbid and nervous and the mental condition has helped to upset the physical.

Compounding Mary's despair was that three friends, including long-time chum Mildred Brown, had become engaged. "Don't I just hope she will be the happiest ever?" Mary wrote on February 23, 1908. "She deserves joy if anybody does. Grace has a lovely diamond. Well heigh ho! Mary Evelyn hasn't and won't cry even if she is lonely. But I'm not!" Another friend, Woody, was also engaged, wrote Mary, who in an aside marveled that she had caught the mumps ("Completed my education at last").

> Woody came back carrying her left hand in her pocket and eating with it under the tablecloth. Tom gave her a little ring for Xmas. Woody is the most amiable creature you ever saw. Honest, she's a dear. And the bed spreads and doilies and napkins and other articles of the "trousseau"—faith! but they are being manufactured with lightning speed. Pillows and collars and chemises and nightcaps and Lord only knows what not . . . ."He" said he loved her and she is wearing his pin and getting lost in dreams of him.

Woody, Mary declared, represented one form of femininity.

> So dainty and sweet, refined and feminine, the clinging vine type, you know, but still with considerable force of character. Enough to have fine ideals and yet not enough to get away from her own SELF. Yes, capitals, please. She is so self-centered, so sensitive, so unaware of the fact that she is only a passing shadow in the lives of nine persons out of ten that she hates their great joys and sorrows, their very struggle for existence totally independent of her. Yet she is not unique in thinking that she is the center of others' lives. It takes such a while for some of us to learn that we aren't half so important in the minds of others as we are in our own . . . that most folks don't notice anything missing if we don't happen to be there.

Mary's funk lifted enough for her to deliver some more literary spunk.

May 10, 1908

Wa'al, Tom and Woody spooning on the couch. Little Mary
lonely as usual. Poor little Mary! Let me shed a few inky tears.
There it is all over now. I've just been eating red rabbit and
drinking coffee strong as Samson and I must do something. Been
to church twice today, disgraced myself tonight by laughing.
There was a vested boys choir, composed mostly of four dear little
red-headed Potters. The elder sister red-haired Potter sat up in the
choir looking down. The boy choir grew hot and Ray Potter got
rid of the hot by peeling his surplico, shirt fashion, over his head.
One after another, the three other warm little Potters followed
suit, and big sister, helpless and horrified, sat in the choir and
gazed at the disrobing in silence. I giggled. Who wouldn't?

Continuing this long entry, Mary recalled collecting mayflowers, her
favorite blossom, with Marian, likely along a path I walked countless
times with Eli and other dogs to the Pawtuckaway River, which forms
the northern border of the Epping property.

One day of days to be remembered when Marian and I went
home and went Maying up by Pawtuckaway stream. Oh, the pink
and white beauties half hidden in the leaves, the brawling stream,
the soft breeze, the balmy air. Then the next day by the meadow
dam, looking up at the blue sky from the foot of the pines. It
is a long look up to those pines. How they swing and sway so
gracefully when the wind blows. And Macduff and Box, the
collies, on guard at head and feet. Such moments are worth living
for. And to think of next summer at the bungalow and day after
day of such life. It seems too good to be true.

(A few years later, Mary offered a perfect canine eulogy after one of
those collies died. "Our dear old Macduff has gone where good dogs
go," she wrote. "I wonder if he has found the one thing to make him
human—the power of speech . . . . He was only a dog but he was a
gentleman of the old school if there ever was one.").

Mary's mood darkened again as she realized that Marian and Osgood had indeed manipulated her.

> July 17, 1909
>
> It is nothing to me that he has fallen in love with her, for he never inspired anything but a friendly interest in me, but to deliberately plan with two other men to keep me "smooth" so that they might work me again this summer for the use of my camp and canoe and a chance to court Marian—I think it is a yellow cur trick and the most outrageous abuse of my hospitality to the whole crowd that they could make. It certainly looks as tho two people whom I have trusted had played their little game without much regard for me, but that is human nature. I can't believe Marian is a party to this conspiracy. And the joke of it is, he would have been ten times more likely to get Marian if he had played a fair game.

Usually confident about her instincts, Mary was upset with herself for misreading Osgood, or at least his intentions.

> But my Lord Chesterfield! Did you ever get left, Mary Evelyn, in your estimate of a man's character? It is sartin a good joke on you. He did fool me completely in my idea of him. But there is one thing to his credit. He judges human nature mighty well. To me he was intellect and impersonal friendliness. He could talk books by the hour and he very cleverly gave me one or two apparent insights into his own character that would make me think him very modest, very chivalrous and very upright . . . . Oh, I thought he was slick!

Maybe Marian was less culpable in sneaking around her, Mary hoped.

> I'll pin my faith on her a bit longer. If it does prove true that she has had a hand in it, I'll just remember that there are other girls who have been loyal friends to me these ten years past. And I'll try to think too, that there are excuses for her—that somehow, something warped her judgment . . . .

There is one thing sure. I've got to do the thing that is right. The only compensation for me in this matter is the knowledge that as far as I know, I have lived up to my ideal of nobility of character . . . . If I let myself down to retaliate I shall have eternally dwarfed my own soul.

Mary had less generous feelings toward Osgood: "Gee! Wouldn't I like to wollop him in a game of chess." She was still stewing as she began a new teaching job in Hopedale, Mass.

March 1, 1910
Say journal, I'm awfully degenerate. I'm not half so good as I used to be. I don't think I am yet a hypocrite, so I carefully inform all my acquaintances that I am degenerated and surely you ought to know it as well. It is just my meh friend, the loyal, true, unselfish, self-sacrificing Marian, and meh other friend, the honorable gentleman, who so chestily declared that for him happiness consisted in right doing have made me so thoroughly sick of the virtues that they have advertised, that I am thinking the opposite vices must be better character makers.

A week later, Mary had perked up. "I feel so hopeful for just these last few days I have felt a peace within myself, a calmness and a strength I've been a stranger to for a year past. I am glad." Alas, that calm "was only a rift in the clouds," Mary wrote next. While disappointed in what she saw as Marian's calculated mercenary motivation for marrying Osgood, she remained more disappointed in her own failure of judgment.

April 22, 1910
Oh why do I have to feel this terrible under-current of bitterness! I never would have believed that I was so weak as to let just one girl's treachery color my vision. But I loved her so well! I believed in her. The colossal selfishness of her has stunned me. And I am so slow to start to feeling anything, and so slow to stop—that now a year after it has happened, there are times when it seems as tho I should die . . . . Oh if she could only have left me

my faith in her! It would have been so easy to have done that.

If she could have even said "I loved him" I could have pitied and forgiven her for I realize that love between woman and man makes great demands. But no, she says, "If he has money enough I intend to marry him" and for that reason, and while she thought that I cared, and that he had given me reason for caring, she encouraged him until he had committed himself in the meantime carefully concealing his attention from me, and pretending that she loved me intensely. And she thought I loved him! My feeling towards him seems such an insignificant factor. I did like him and I did have a great respect for him until I found him out, but I knew him about two weeks and he seems like an unreal vision now, but Marian I loved better than myself for three good years of my life.

Despite wanting to move on, Mary was still angry more than a year later on October 27, 1911, as she recalled a summer visit from "me deah Marian . . .

> . . . to 'celebrate our anniversary in the place of our first meet', as she [said]. I'm afraid I was unchristian. The memory of her would-be treachery came up and choked me, and while I don't wish her anything more than she deserves and am willing to let Nemesis give it to her, I just couldn't be decent. So I cut her dead. I'd like never to see her. I loved her so well and she loved me so little. We never have much use for the folks we get sold over.

By the time Mary wrote that entry, Marian Snyder and Clinton Osgood had married. Marian's Congregational minister father officiated at the wedding on August 18, 1910, in Chicopee, Mass. On that same date, Mary entered a long poem into her journal, with this opening stanza.

> I'm lonely now in Arcady
>   Strange to say
> For the merry crowd has flitted
>   Far away.
> Tho the waters still do murmur

On the shore
Tho the stately pines still whisper
Woodland lore
Yet I'm sad in Arcady
Just Today
For I miss the friendly faces
Gone away.

"Where are your dreams of a year ago?"

Just as the deaths of young mates and her sister Mabel threw Mary into tailspins, the end of things with male suitors Will and Ralph and then with Marian made Mary even more depressed about her relationship prospects. "This being a disgruntled old maid is not all it's cracked up to be," she groused to her journal. She also anguished over the deaths of her uncle George and her sister Mabel's seven-year-old son Fred Perry.

December 7, 1908
I've been troubled by something not real. The only "real" ones are death and sickness and disgrace. Alas, the former has come to me to show how dwarfed all other griefs are by its mighty shadow. Freddie has left us. He sleeps on the hillside by his mother and I sometimes think of her as no longer being alone but with one of her babies clasped in her long-empty arms and the ache of her mother heart stilled by the companionship of a fair son. But, oh our hearts ache. He was such a beautiful, lovable boy. Had he lived to be an old man, serving his fellow citizens all his days, no greater grief could have been shown at his departure. The old and the young followed the little white casket in sorrow and with many tears . . . .

Uncle George died this fall and Auntie has gone way out to West Port, leaving her home shut up. I pity her from the bottom of my heart. It must be such a wrench to bar oneself from the home of the long married years, of early childhood, of friends, and that saddest and perhaps dearest of earthly possessions—a new made grave.

Mary was in better spirits a few weeks later and wanted to chronicle "a joyful fall before it is dimmed in my memory." Her eloquence about the natural world shined as she wrote of an autumn hike to High Rock, a four-hundred-foot hill in Foxboro led by Oscar, "a small Swede, who is one of Miss Johnson's pupils."

> Oscar armed himself with a rabbit dog, a long string whereon to tie the rabbits that he expected to catch and two bottles of sour warm wine wherewith to cool his parched throat. He was a few inches taller than his dog and with his white big hat resting firmly on his ears made quite a picture of himself. I had visions of the dignified Miss Johnson and myself marching thru the streets of Foxboro fairly laden down with rabbits.

The troupe had dinner "perched on the top of a high gray ledge, looking down into the maze of tangled growth aglow with transparent yellows and vivid scarlets of the maples and rich with the golden brown of new fallen pine needles."

> Up farther in Highrock proper, piled with great rocks and upheaved ledges, the scrub oak had found a foothold and lit up the scene with vivid carmine. After noon found us on the edge of a young hardwood growth where the slanting southern sunbeams shone with almost summer warmth. The leaves had partly fallen and every gust sent down others swirling thru the air. They had filled a deep hollow, making it the most comfortable of resting places. I curled up in it and watched the down falling leaves and listened to the noisy chattering of the birds' congress next door, met to discuss their autumnal trip.
>
> As I looked and listened the hazy misty air grew hazier, the bird chorus fainter and far away, and I slept a modern Babe in the Woods on the breast of the great mother from whose arms we cannot long stay away, waking refreshed and ready for the homewood jaunt.

While relishing the real world of leaves and birds, Mary remained intrigued by a less discernible domain.

> March 1909
> There are paths I may not tread, depths I can not seek, vistas my eyes can never fathom, but while life lasts I can seek farther, new facts, new wonders—oh, there is no end. Thou most glorious unknown! And in the end Death opens a gate into the greatest of all the great unknowns where there is more time to seek. When I shall be in correspondence with that outer environment, that men call God. Perhaps, then this veil that hides from me the beauty that I would see will be removed. This horrible veil—this maddening veil. You have seen people move behind a curtain whose folds show in strange distortions some outline of their forms. Dim, indistinct, distorted and unreal, yet you know that life exists there.

Mary wondered what "unknown world" lay beyond "this intangible gray, drifting curtain."

> Is it the fairy realm of fancy, where poets dwell? Will [the veil] ever be lifted for me? Sometimes I half fancy that it will when I shall have known the mountain peaks and the valley of the Shadow. When Experience will have branded on my mentality in letters of searing flame "Real."

Perhaps that parallel universe is home to the children that, in a lifelong lament, Mary so wished could be her own.

> I sometimes think that those dim shapes that half show their forms of beauty from behind the curtain are the children that I might bring forth to name me by the sacred name. But since I cannot call them forth alone they seem extremely likely to stay there. I wonder if these voiceless longings that tear me so would find expression in a future generation and give to the world the

real things that exist behind the veil. I cannot interpret. I can only
<u>feel</u>, but since I feel perchance a future generation will have the
power denied me.

It may be it is Death who holds down the veil, and when he
lifts it I shall pass on to join the vanishers into the unknown.
Methinks there is some terror in this Unknown—no, not if there
is faith—and love—for perfect love casteth out fear.

Mary did not return to her journal until it was time for her annual
birthday reflection. She labeled this entry "The Bungalow," indicating
that she had not yet christened her camp "Arcady." Even in its "peace of
the pines," Mary was far from tranquil as she lamented dreams lost.

> July 8, 1909
> Twenty eight years old! Well, when all is said and done where
> are the visions of ten years ago? You have done nothing that you
> intended to do. As far as that goes, where are your dreams of a year
> ago? Do you remember a year ago today? The sky was blue and the
> little white clouds went scudding across it and you thought it just
> your day. Your heart was light and your step free and joy went with
> you. Your day, oh—your day! My faith it was a short one. Today
> the skies are blue and the white clouds scud across but something
> of the joy of living has been taken from you, and it seems as tho
> the old elasticity were gone forever. I can't describe it. There was a
> lifting of my heart when the wind blew upon me or the sun shone
> upon me that was the purest and the cleanest joy that heart can
> know. And now—there's a twilight at noontime.
> Oh Brace Up Quick.

"I've braced!" Mary reported days later. Determined to move past
Marian and Osgood, she hoped for her darker moods to brighten.

> July 17, 1909
> I just had the jim-jams, Journal dear. There are lots of off-sets
> that compensate. Really there isn't so very much reason for having

the blues. It certainly looks as tho two people whom I have trusted had played their little game without much regard for me, but that is human nature.

I begin to think there are hopes for me, journal. I believe these March winds are going to blow me thru and thru and help to clean away the malice and suspicion that have built their rookeries in me. I feel so hopeful for just these last few days I have felt a peace within myself, a calmness and a strength I've been a stranger to for a year past.

A new and very friendly soul was buoying Mary's fresh hope.

Chapter 7

Anne of Arcady

The deep and lasting relationship between Mary Evelyn Folsom and Anne Reed was interwoven with another piece of Mary's bedrock: Arcady, her lakeside sanctuary.

As I wrote in the introduction, I'd been able to locate Arcady but I had just about given up on learning much more about one of its most important guests, Anne Reed. I drew most of what I knew of the Anne-Mary relationship from Mary's journals, in which Anne merited more space than any other person, including Edmond. But then I found that envelope with the 1917 Arkansas postmark, leading me to Anne Reed's great grandson, who in turn introduced me to his mother, who had a stash of her grandmother Anne's letters, including a few from Mary. Those letters, the journals, and recollections from people who knew Mary and Anne helped me piece together this chapter. So too did Arcady itself, where the relationship still lives in faded writings inscribed over several decades onto doors and walls. It was here Mary bestowed upon her dear friend the *nom de camp*, "Anne of Arcady."

With all this material, I thought I had the Anne-Mary story pretty well figured out: The two became close friends when both were teaching in Massachusetts. Their bonds grew during summers together at Arcady—until Anne met the man she would eventually marry, turning her into Anne of Arkansas in 1914. As had happened with Marian, Mary lost a woman close to her to one of Arcady's gentle knights. But while Mary declared Marian "dead to me" after her betrayal, she could not, would not, drop Anne Reed. Now I began to see two Marys. In the privacy of her journals, one Mary was open about her loss and longing. But when writing to Anne and Anne's family, a second Mary wore an outwardly happier face. She was determined to keep at least some part of Anne of Arcady alive.

Mary's first journal mention of Anne Reed came in the same April 22, 1910, entry in which she vented about Marian. Though hopeful about new friend Anne, Mary was wary of entering into another relationship, regardless of gender.

The shattering of my faith in [Marian] seems to have shattered the mainspring in myself. I mean to mend it up. I realize that if I can only love someone else hard enough it will help. But I am just clean scared to try. And loving isn't the easy matter it used to be with me. I can see faults in most everyone.

I do find much consolation in Anne Reed for she seems sincere and true, and her mind is so good and her opinions very wise for so young a body. I think in a way I could care more for her than for Marian even, for I never have to apologize for her, feel ashamed of her, or explain away the doubtfulness of her actions three things that I got well trained for Marian. But oh dear, I'm scared to try. I'd even try loving some man if I could if it would do any good and I was sure he wouldn't know and he was decent enough so I wouldn't feel ashamed of him. But I haven't seen anyone I thought ideal enough for such medicinal purposes this many a long day.

Anne Reed would fill that prescription.

"You may expect nothing but rhapsodies, plans, dreams, and visions."

Seven years younger than Mary, Anna Frances Reed was born in Lexington, Mass., on September 29, 1888. The two women met around 1910 when Mary was teaching in Hopedale, Mass., while Anne was in a school about twenty-five miles away in Hudson, Mass. According to the 1910 U.S. Census, Anne lived with her parents and four siblings in Waltham, Mass., while Mary was a "lodger" in Hopedale.

The two soon enjoyed time with each other. Besides sharing a profession, their fathers were farmers (Mary's raised livestock and hay on the ancestral Epping homestead; Anne's was a truck farmer in Waltham.). These thoughtful women were drawn to each other's intellects and independent spirits in an era when women were beginning to pursue their own careers and lives.

Anne and Mary escaped their classrooms and residential confines to attend theater and other cultural and social events. "Do you know I am just crazy to see Ben Hur? They say it is better this year than it has ever been before," Mary wrote Anne on March 3, 1910. "I've no desire to sit by my lonesome off somewhere else so I thought you perhaps could keep me company. It is my treat, understand, and I shant be seized with a fit of bashfulness and let you interview the agent this time."

About two weeks later, Mary, using her initials, accepted an invitation from Anne. "Your program appeals to M.E. 'Within the Law' will be well worth seeing." (The reference is likely to a play by Bayard Veiller.). Their bonds to each other deepening, Mary wrote that she was eager for the end of the school year and the start of summer, especially one at Arcady with her close chum.

> April 5, 1910
> There are lots of other folks I really ought to write to worser but some how or other I want to write to you morer. I have my plans fairly well developed for going into camp the 21st of June, the Thursday after my school closes. The moon fulls the twenty second so there will be a night or two of "the moon, bright breathless and buoyant and brimful of June" when we can paddle round in the wee small hours. For the next ten weeks you may expect nothing but rhapsodies, plans, dreams, and visions.
> As before ... I love you   Mary Evelyn

I was again struck by Mary's literary reservoir, that she could so readily recall that line about the moon from *Lucile*, a verse novel written by Owen Meredith in 1860. Unlike Mary, who at that point had no formal education beyond high school, Anne received two years of teacher training at Framingham Normal School in Massachusetts (now Framingham State University). But with years of hard classroom experience behind her, Mary offered lessons about classroom decorum to the less experienced Anne in a November 21, 1910, letter. Today, Mary would be sanctioned or worse for how she handled ...

> ... a little imp who kept me [at school] two hours. I'd told him that he might take his choice between doing some work I gave him or staying until I was ready to go home. He was a fifth grade boy, hence my giving him a choice. He wasn't going to do either.

I hung on to his fine young shirt. Said shirt tore. Then he tried
the jiu-jitsu act. I picked him up and swung him round my hip
two or three times and told him I knew more jiu jitsu than he
did. He was going to sail in and lay me out. I let him sail until he
got tired and then I remarked urbanely that I was sorry he wasn't
any bigger for if I had got to have a fight it would make it more
interesting to have some one nearer my size! James was very
much crestfallen at my serenity and decided that he would wait
even as I directed . . . . I never had such a fuss. He wasn't one of
mine either but he'll probably come to me next year and I had
to conquer or die.

Anne and Mary relished being free from the usual all at Arcady. "One
night Anne and I fled away from the dishes, a common occurrence, to
float in our canoe into the heart of a golden sunset," Mary wrote in her
journal on August 18, 1910. "After it had faded we drifted about under
the stars talking of many things and wondering if our fleeing from duty
to seek the sunset splendor was typical of Life. Pleasure is so fleeting, but
it leaves such joyful memories."

Far from work and, for the most part, civilization, Arcady was a refuge
for free spirits. "Ah how many stories those pines have in their holding!"
Mary wrote. "Anne and I were talking about love last night. We—I guess
I was talking last night about Love to Anne. That's it. Anne is a canny
child who looks unutterably wise over deep questions like this."

Though intrigued by Anne, Mary still partook in the flirtations that
were the order of the Arcady day.

6. Photo in journal shows Mary, left, and Anne doing "a little highly civilized picnicking."

August 19, 1910

There has been another summer at Arcady to get on record and on the whole it has been the most joyful one yet . . . . We went to a dance or two, and Ruth got in some deadly work on Don Leddy's fine young heart. Really they became quite devoted. I used to ask Don if he didn't want to hold my hand for a change but he never seemed to want to.

Over the Fourth the boys . . . came up and with them my dear Anne Reed, looking very sweet and demure with her four gallant escorts. That first night in a fit of mistaken wisdom I put all four of the boys out on the piazza, thinking they would enjoy sleeping outdoors. Sleeping! Ye Gods! Not one wink slept we— except Johnnie, who slept audible like except when I stood over her and held her mouth together. Anne and I fled away in the early dawn down the lake in search of sweet repose. She found a wee bit, but not a wink did I, "alas for me".

They slept a bit better the next night "thanks to a wiser distribution of the boys," the entry continued. And Anne was attracting male attention.

> [T]he next night we rode over to Raymond to a dance . . .
> in a hayrack and 'twas very jolty. In spite of it all, I think most of
> us went to sleep coming home except Billy and I were just doing a
> little missionary work, I were, sort er reclining on Billy's shoulder
> just distracting his attention from thinking too much about
> whether Leonard was supporting Anne properly or not. Poor
> Billy: he has had a Platonic friendship with Anne all winter and it
> was pretty tough to see another fellow have the innings. I felt very
> sorry for him. I guess I had a queer way of showing it tho. I invited
> Marian Wiggin up, and stored Billy away on the back seat between
> her and Anne where he looked thoroughly wretched . . . .
>   I deposited me own rose bud mouth about three inches below
> Billy's chin, and back of his head I placed a pillow that he had
> to hold firmly against the rail or 'twould fall out. So when Billy
> would have fallen into the natural follies of mankind, and bent his
> head, away started the kindly pillow from tumbling out. It did go
> once, and Billy said "Damn" thereby waking up the other sleepers,
> and he had to hike after it. It was lots of fun. I did enjoy it. It was
> like poking your fingers into a cat's ribs and trying to haul them
> out before he clawed you. Thanks to my forethought in arranging
> the pillow I won the game.

Mary missed Anne after she returned to her job in Massachusetts. "When I entered the lonely camp and looked across to where their white tent had stood, and saw on the floor a scrap of my green dress, the ache was considerable. It drove me to poetry, the next thing to drink." The poem Mary wrote into her journal had these opening and closing stanzas.

> Straight in the path of the setting sun
>   Anne and I together
> Floating out in our little canoe
>   Light as an eagle's feather . . . .

Tho all the sunset glories flee
And rough and dark the weather
Fast in my heart are those golden days
When Anne and I were together.

7. Mary (in the stern) and Anne Reed (bow) paddle by Arcady.

In an undated photograph, Mary and Anne are canoeing on the Pawtuckaway, with Mary in the stern and an unidentified woman sitting in the middle. All three women have their hair neatly tied up. They wear dresses that seem pristine and dry, certainly not canoe-friendly by today's measure.

Mary, who had met some of Anne's New Hampshire family, recapped a happy summer in an October 18, 1910, letter to Anne. "I did have the bestest time, Anne. It seemed so good to see you again and I am so glad to have met your people. I hope they like me as well as I do them." By then, Mary and Anne were back in their Massachusetts schools. "The summer time is just a memory now and the day's work is present," Mary wrote in her journal on November 3, 1910. "My faith! Why do I like the day's play so much better?"

Unbeknownst to the hostess of Arcady, another of Arcady's "gentle Knights of the Tent" was about to turn Anne of Arcady into Anne of Arkansas.

Mary had mentioned a visitor named Downs in her journal, writing that she'd like to know him better though she did not expect that to happen. "Anne, dear heart" remained atop Mary's thoughts. "Remember, the Saturday after the Saturday after Thanksgiving is for thee and me," she wrote in a November 21, 1910, letter, signing it, "I love thee. M.E." About a month later, Mary urged Anne to apply for a teaching vacancy in Hopedale. The position "ought to pay from $14 to $16 a week" (just over $400 a week in current dollars), Mary wrote.

> We could room and board together, oh joy! I haven't much idea of such joy but I wish it might be . . . . I stayed awake until midnight last night dreaming of the joyful times we would have if you judged it wise to come. I have much fear that you won't. It would be too good to be true. With much love and some few rosy dreams that I expect will be smashed. Lovingly, M.E.

Days later, Mary reacted to a photograph Anne had sent of herself. "Your face looks at me sweetly and sedately as it has a habit of doing when the original is present. Your picture was such a delightful surprise . . . . I shall keep it to look at when I get the blues or feel 'degenerate' for it will remind me that there are some mighty good things in the world—even if they take up very little room!"

In a letter in which Mary was prescient about making holiday observance dates more practical, Mary was anxious for Anne to join her in Hopedale.

> February 17, 1911
> How I wish Washington's birthday came always on a Monday or a Friday. It would be so convenient for us poor school marms . . . . Only five weeks more to teach and then you will be coming to keep me company . . . . When you get to Hopedale I shall take just the best care of you and give you massages when you can't sleep and if you start in on a cold I'll know just how to break it up.

"Anne, dear heart, is at last teaching in Hopedale," Mary rejoiced in her journal on April 22, 1911. But she also noted, with some resentment if not outright jealousy, that the same Dick Downs that Mary had so fleetingly noted a few months earlier was on his way to see Anne.

> Anne had a letter from Dick, one of our summer acquaintances yesterday, saying that he was going to arrive in Boston Friday and should "expect" to hear from her. "Wore" she aviated over that "expect." "What business had he to 'expect' anything". He is a nice lad just the same. Maybe when she gets to be "this side of forty" — like me—if a man does "expect" something she won't mind. I think I'd rather like it.

Ralph Aaron King Downs, also known as Dick, was born in Berwick, Maine, on April 19, 1885. He and Anne apparently met at Arcady during that summer of 1910; Mary's list of visitors on the back of Arcady's door for that year included, "Dick who has a large heart—a glass heart—a heart bound with silver!"

Perhaps Mary, who appeared to be impressed with Dick's intellect and character, wanted him to be more than just an acquaintance. Maybe she even told him so, based on a postcard from Dick to Mary on April 25, 1911, almost a year after the door inscription. Addressed "to Miss M.E. Folsom" and bearing a Moscow, Ark., postmark, the note from "Ralph D." contained just this short, cryptic message: "(Why this silence?) I guess you must have forgotten what you used to tell me last summer." Had Mary given Dick cause to expect something more from her? Was Mary resentful that Dick was intruding on her relationship with Anne—or was she upset that Dick was less interested in her? That piece of my Mary jigsaw puzzle remains missing.

"Gee! I was lonesome—nobody loves M.E."

As she turned thirty-one on July 8, 1912, Mary remained attached to Anne, but she also enjoyed relationships—or maybe just toying—with certain men, including the Raymondites, as she dubbed the lads who visited Arcady from that town five miles away. Perhaps seeking more than friendship, Mary feared that her behavior drove away potential suitors.

July 8, 1912

I'm afraid our happy quintette is finished. Leonard and
Castilo are off the hooks. Roe moves to town and I feel a
melancholy satisfaction in predicting his speedy marriage to
some damsel who won't care for the old friend. Oh-Gee. I get
sick of these jolly crowds parting . . . . I feel it in my bones that
Roe and I will see or hear little of each other. I carried my teasing
too far and now he's disgusted and it's Goodbye Wesley. Same
old story. I ought not let my love of teasing take me so far.

As a new year began, Mary was feeing low as she reflected on the
death of her sister.

Jan 1ˢᵗ 1913

13! Unlucky year. I hope the feeling of dread towards its
gifts is not a fore-runner of evil. I certainly have a horrible
down-cast feeling. Let me cultivate fortitude and serenity,
high ideals and charity.

Oh bah. I'm afraid I'm going to pieces. Nine years ago.
Providence has a strange way of doing things. What a lot
of things she might have done and how little I have. I've no
business living. God almighty makes awful mistakes sometimes.

Mary's mood may have been darkened by her growing suspicions that
something was afoot with Anne—something that did not include her.
The full reveal came a month later in an entry Mary pegged to lessons
gleaned from *The Garden of Allah*. (Rather than the stage version, Mary
likely saw the silent movie of a play based on Robert Hichens's 1904
novel about a British woman who had an affair with a fallen Trappist
monk.). Mary began this February 3, 1913, entry with the broader
lessons she drew.

Well Journal, interesting communications I have to make. I
went to see the Garden of Allah Saturday. Rather a splendid
spectacle. More-over I rather think I know how to sympathize
with Boris. There's such a thing as working up to the realization of

the meaning of one's womanhood when it's too late. Incidentally I drew a highly ethical lesson from one of Count Antioni's speeches. He thinks of Antoine as being very wicked because he has broken his priestly vows, yet he, Antioni, is a better and nobler man for having listened to his words of faith and love.

Then Mary turned to "my application" of these lessons to her own situation. Dick and Anne were engaged. Mary saw it as a mismatch—one that left Mary in "Lonely Land."

I went out to Anne's and found her with a large Diamond of Dick's adorning her finger. Gee! talk about your surprises. She has always found Dick as great a subject of mirth . . . and yet she is going to marry. Well, love is queer. He's a nice clean fellow, and I know he'll get along in the world. She will have all manner of creature comforts I am sure. I feel qualms about the rest. As I remember Dick he cares little for the things she likes. I behaved like a blooming fool, which of course is a great consolation—always is. I hate to lose her. And lose her I must. She has meant a great deal to me these last few years. I've loved her very dearly and I've burdened her with my woes and at least tried to share my pleasures with her. I guess perhaps I've inflicted both a little too much. She certainly has helped me thru some tough places. I realize I'm taking a terribly selfish view of it. I ought to be thinking only of her happiness but it's tough to walk all alone in Lonely land, and tho it is my own fault, that is cold comfort. I reckon too that my self love is a bit wounded.

Worse, Mary continued, Anne shared the news of her engagement with others long before she told her beloved Mary.

Her three months friends in Winthrop knew about it sometime ago. Last week I went to Foxboro and . . . she took off her ring for my benefit. I felt something, but thought I was having a spell of imagination. It does seem queer that I should be the last to know, when I'm the only one to know Dick, and really had flattered myself that I was a "here-friend." Well, cheer up . . . now she has Dickie she doesn't need me. And I?—Well, I'm going alone—my own road—alone. No more opening of heart and soul that he who runs may read. I'll try to make other folks happy.

The application? Evidently I do make other folks happy. Think of Marian and Anne both owing their happiness to M.E. . . . . Well, with all my successes in other folks joys, you haven't exactly heard me howling with my own have you?

Pensive at Arcady, Mary accepted the end of her days to be remembered with Anne. In a photograph pasted opposite this entry (the picture is on the frontispiece and cover of this book), Mary sits alone at a wooden table under the tall pines, pen poised over her journal. Holding that same leather-bound journal at Arcady one day, I glance over to where Mary sat at water's edge for that photographic moment.

> July 28, 1913
> I do look so serene and calm. I can share the irony of the gods and show a peace I do not feel, a strength I haven't got, a purity that I strive for, but being very human fall far short of. I know I've reverted this summer. Never mind. I've enjoyed the reversion. I think I'll continue to revert. What's the use. Quien sabe. I wonder what's ended! Am I? Well, I'm not afraid.
>
> Well, Journal dear, I'm coming to the last entries on your pages for I know that the story of this summer will fill them. And I have a strange feeling that I have written "It is ended" after some of my life. I wonder what it means—what is ended? My Anne and I have had our last dreams together here—next year it will be Dick's Anne—not mine . . . . I don't know what is "ended." Maybe the old good times in Arcady . . . . Maybe my own dreams. That's right. Ha-ha.

Mary was especially shattered to see one of her most special dreams—to have her own children—at its apparent end, even as what she saw as less worthy mothers have them.

Why am I made the way I am. The far high gods must shout with ironic laughter at the microscopic struggle of the ants down here. Why not laugh too—laugh and ask nothing of them. They take me and send thru my veins this love of living—the joy of life—until I thrill like a harp in the wind and flame like the pitchy cones I fling to the fire and they give me the knowledge of what it means and the power to hold myself clean and a heart that loves little children, "then" they take some clinging vine whose lips are common property and to her they give a mate whose children she most reluctantly bears fearful lest she loses her figure and moaning because she is "tied down." And she becomes the mother of the race—and I have Mary Folsom spinster on my grave-stone. Sometime I wish that epitaph might be soon written—Bah.

Mary's hurt and resignation continued to show a couple of weeks in a letter to Anne, who had made a visit.

August 12, 1913

It's nice of you to stop in the midst of your happiness and think of sharing it with M.E. I sometimes find myself sorely rebellious at the prospect of the end of the sharing but I suppose I ought to be very grateful for all that has been. I are! Only—there will never be anyone else. And there is something tells me rather definitely that the solace that most girls find when their girl-friends get married—that sincerest flattery—imitation—is not in my line. Heigh-ho—well—all signs fail in a dry time.

The letter went on to describe visits, flirting, and other goings-on with the old crowd at Arcady. Mary wrote as if everything was still the same with Anne before returning to her grim present.

Gee! I was lonesome—nobody loves M.E. The last night they were there I stayed out on the piazza and entertained them until they ought to have been sleepy enough to go to bed. I was. But I had to succumb! I slept under the window there so I took the owl—since nothing better presented—and with it clasped tenderly in my arms proceeded to slumber.

Anne Reed and Ralph Downs married in Berwick, Maine, on June 15, 1914. The couple moved to Arkansas, where Downs had found work as a cotton broker. (Anne's granddaughter told me that Ralph was steered to that job by someone he met while working as a bellboy at a hotel in Maine.). After Anne's wedding, the two Marys—the first inwardly miserable and the other outwardly cheery—became more apparent. Writing to Anne's mother, Mary was upbeat in describing the wedding, in which she was a participant (along with the cat Walloper), something Mary did not even mention in her journal. The letter's tone masked its writer's private pain.

> Dear Mrs. Reed
> I suppose Joe [Mrs. Reed's brother] has told you all about
> Anne's wedding from the masculine standpoint, but maybe you
> would like to hear about it from the feminine side. We found
> Dick in Dover, somewhat surprised at seeing me but I told him,
> seeing as I was so responsible, I felt obliged to see them thru ....
> Everybody thought I was the blooming bride. I did my best. I
> looked coy and blushing and happy! Those who saw him with
> a brown and black sort of a female will be surprised next to see
> him with a blue and white one. Mrs. Downs and his sister looked
> astonished enough when Dick handed me out. They were very
> cordial and kindly.
> Anne was married in the little parlor of their home. The
> minister's daughter played the wedding march and someone gave
> Anne a bunch of roses . . . . She looked very lovely and sweet and
> Dick looked very proud and happy, altho he did get rattled on
> 'With this ring I thee wed'.
> There were present only his mother and sister, Joe and I,
> the minister and his daughter, a little girl who found some light
> refreshments and oh yes "Walloper." He can't lose him I
> hope you'll try to get up this summer. I want you to meet my
> mother. She sends you her love.

Within the sanctity of her journal, however, Mary would spill out her true feelings about Anne of Arcady becoming Anne of Arkansas.

Chapter 8

Farewell to Anne of Arcady

Mary began the fourth and final volume of "her book" about two months before the wedding of Anne Reed. "Even as before," she inscribed on the cover page, noting that her "18th year of the writing of journals" was "Begun on April 6, 1914" and "Ended—God knows—".

8. Mary begins her "strange sort of an engagement present" to Anne.

Mary filled nearly half of this inch-thick brown notebook with a single, melancholy section titled "Idylls of Arcady," dedicated to "the little sister of my heart," Anne of Arcady, "lest she forget." What followed was page after page of prose and poetry, beginning with a long letter "to Anne of Arcady before she becomes Anne of Arkansas." The "letter" was eloquent, at times intimate—but was it ever sent? Nothing like it was in the collection of correspondence held by Anne's granddaughter. I suspect that a forlorn Mary never intended to send this letter, that she penned it as an emotional release for herself. Mailed or not, this extraordinary passage captured the depth of the bonds and the "memories to be recalled" for these two women.

This was Mary at full emotional and literary strength—"It's a bit of myself I'm giving to your keeping."

> Anne, dear Heart
>
> This is a strange sort of an engagement present but I'm sure you'll have no other like it. It's to Anne of Arcady before she becomes Anne of Arkansas. Arcady has woven its sunlight and shadow and silvery nights and flitting fogs into your life in such an intimate sort of a way—for had you not been first of Arcady, you had not been secondly of Arkansas—that I am thinking for a little while you'll like all reminder of it. Then this epistle can find its place into some old chest, and very properly be forgotten.
>
> Forgotten! Until some day another blue-eyed Anne will run across it and say, "Mother, what's the meaning of all this faded print and erratic writing, this yellowed paper and near-poetry?" Then, oh—then, dear heart, you will remember! Whatever may have come between you will remember. You will float again with me into the heart of the golden sunset, you'll follow the mountain road, winding thru the upland valley to the top of old Pawtuckaway, you'll drift in the noon of night, silent under the stars, and listen to the voices of the night . . . .
>
> You'll remember how the pine tops looked like feathery ferns against the dear twilight of the upper air when we lay at their base wrapped in our blankets, and gazed up along their tapering trunks into illimitable space where the lone stars dwell.
>
> You'll remember our nights on the Point of Pines, alone, the earth for our pillow, the heavens for a canopy, you'll feel the thrill of wonder when that deepest darkness just before the dawn lightens, and the bird chorus begins its matin-song. You'll see the bank of cloud low-lying in the east, shot thru with flaming arrows, and the eastern heavens aglow with fiery splendor. You'll watch the naughty mist-spirits go flying down the lake for one last mad whirling dance before their great father, the sun, draws them to him-self.

Mary began to transition from these idyllic memories to her unwitting role in losing Anne.

Thou and I, my Anne, have sought joyously for the adventures
of Life, without fear, either of convention, or of bugs, or—
perhaps another synonym of convention—our fellow men. Because
we've had no fear of bugs we've nestled contentedly on the lap
of mother earth and learned some wisdom thereby. And because
we've had no over-fear of convention we have shaken hands with
Romance—at least you have. I am the one who watches. I am the
one who forms the Background. And yet you were presented to
Dick with due form and ceremony were you not. But methinks
there was something unconventional at that. Never did I dream
that in one of our gentle Knights of the Tent and Ashen Blade you
would find your young Lochinvar out of the West. I would not
have played the part of blinded Fate so meekly had I known, for
Arkansas is two thousand and one miles too far away.

Anne and Mary thrived not just at Arcady but in Bohemia, Mary continued.

In fact I think we may call Arcady the Forest of Arden in the
Kingdom of Bohemia. No! That will never do, for they are
independent countries after all. There may be slums and dark
places in Bohemia—leper spots under the jewels. There's none of
that in Arcady. There are, instead, dryads and Pan and fairies and,
best of all, an Enchanted Isle [that] always has a blue sky over it
and sparkling waters around it and the wind sings strange melodies
thru its trees . . . ah, 'tis then a fairy isle, a spot to dream in—to live
in—to love in while life is young and the red blood of youth flows
warmly in our veins . . . .

Thanks be to whatever gods there are for that lure of the
unknown that's ever haunting us—the strange faith that beckons
with a mysterious strength. It's the greatest joy of life to master
some new thing, and surely when at last the great adventure
looms before us, Death will only be the gateway of a greater
unknown where there's just more room for exploration.

Mary wanted Anne to cling to memories of their "happy lot" even as
they become separated by half a continent.

You'll not forget all our long and serious and sedate discussions of every subject underneath the sun, and some we new invented. You'll think of the nights when we loved the fireplace best and curled up in Oriental luxury before it.

I can not teach these clumsy fingers of mine to fashion dainty things of shining silks and white linen, but I've tried to fashion here some memories to be recalled on rainy days when there's nothing else to do. The fine linen would have been for all to see, but this must be only for those who have that understanding heart. . . . Since in Arcady there are some shadows, which make the sunlight brighter, you will forgive the bits of sombreness which may show thru, here and there. They too are part of me.

It has been our happy lot to follow together so many winding roads, flecked with sunshine, sprinkled with shadow, when the sky was blue and the little white clouds went scudding by "When all the world's a vibrant harp—The winds of God have strung". Now our roads lie far apart and it "greets me sair."

There ought nothing of regret creep into anything we give a bride-to-be, but oh, little sister of my heart how can I help it when that, too, is very much a part of me.

I'm glad we've had so much of gypsying—to paraphrase "When we had heart for hazarding, When we had will to dare." Now take these wee bit reminders of the days that have been to amuse yourself a bit in the days that are to be.

M.E.

Those "wee bit reminders" were mainly poems themed to Arcady, the natural world, spiritualism, Bohemian freedom, and mythology. After a poem "To Morpheus", the Greek god of sleep and dreams ("Hold me fast in peaceful sleep/Free from all alarms"), Mary returned to prose as she continued her Idylls of Arcady.

How often are the beginnings of tragedy "trifles light as air." Poor little maid whose frail dancing feet have dared too long the edge of the chasm—and yet I do not believe her pathway led along the edge long enough for her to look over and fear the depths. More likely she wove her garlands of dreams and fluttered about in the meadow with the other butterflies until the chasm yawned so suddenly that her feet slipped over before she ever dreamed of the gulf before.

I'm glad she dreamed for a little space in Arcady.

Most people would dismiss such mythical thoughts and magical moments, Mary wrote. But not Anne.

There were the still nights when the drifting fogs arose in all the little quiet coves and we, gliding steadily among them, saw strange fantastic doings that we'd be laughed at outside for telling. But I've been half afraid to dance the midnight out since for fear I'll be coming back a hundred years or so to be one of those dim dancing creatures that we've half glympsed so many times.

After more verse, Mary resumed her prose, linking her love of the natural world with the supernatural one and her visions as a "priestess of Pan."

You know I'm half pagan all the time and seven eighths some of the time. In the old days when I was a priestess of Pan I never wove down a woodland glade without an insane and wild desire to fling my arms over my head and dance and sway to the cadence of strange music that is unlawful for the 1/8 of me to hear. Before me the little people move aside and back of me they close in together only opposite they get still and quiet and I can't quite see them. They're afraid of the 1/8 of me that still isn't pagan. However their rustling and whisperings are plain to my ear tho their forms are veiled to my sight. When I shake the 1/8 off I shall see them.

And why should it be all nonsense? Is there no soul to all the lovely inanimate things that whisper to us and sing to us and fill us with awe and amazement unspeakable. Anteus arose from contact with his mother earth, renewed in vigor, tireless, unconquerable. So may we, if we let not some terrible modern Hercules of haste and worry and desire for manmade things choke out of us this love of the great mother and her gifts of life. When we are weary of the little ways of little folks she lets us fling ourselves upon her breast and be comforted. How mothering and kindly she looks upon us—her children.

Then comes spring, which brings "a bit of calm to live in."

The snows are gone, the little brooks run wild, every twig is dripping wet and every bud is swelling with the promise of new life within. It is before the time of singing bird and opening flower, but the soil is black and rich and heavy with the promise of fertility to come. It is the time of sacred mysteries when the seed that has lain dormant in the womb of mother earth thru the long winter months quickens to life.

There are premonitions everywhere, of all the beauty that is to be—dreams of the ecstatic songs of birds and flowers in bloom and the wild joys of June. It is small wonder that the blood of men and women thrill in subtle sympathy with these great forces of nature.

Mary was glad she "served at the altars of Pan, Pan of the untrimmed forests and the deep mountain lake and the untrodden moor. The master and protector of all the little forest folk. He who plays on the harp of the wind and pipes thru the throats of the birds." Her fascination with this Greek god lives in a long poem she wrote into her journal that also covers most of an Arcady wall. "I have danced to the sound of thy piping/I have followed the lure of thy song," the poet declares.

> O you, who tamely sit beside your warm hearth fire
> And shiver at the wild call of the wintry wind
> You never know the fierce and wild desire
> The exultant rush of flame
> Thru every vein to finger tips
> When once you've answered to the trumpet call,

Heeded by few, tho heard by all
The insistent "Home? Home!" of the wind.

"I'm sorry that I cannot keep my meter regular like but spring and winter is two such different folks," added Mary as she began to wind down her long farewell to Anne and to their times together. "To be sure there's little filthy lucre to our credit in the banks of the nation, but think of all our riches in the banks of memory."

There was for me an undercurrent of sadness—perhaps for thee for thou and I, my Anne, have dreamed our last dreams together under the pines. Next year it will be Dick's Anne, not mine, and our dreams will be far apart.

The peace of the pines be with thee
The memory of days of ease
Of shimmering sun on the water
Of whispering winds on the trees.

In the days that are to be when your Test of Little Things arise before you and you do not call them blessed you will remember the halcyon days by peaceful Pawtuckaway, an isle of calm set round by troubled seas. And when my Test confronts me—the Temptation from within—I'll pray that something of the strength of these great pines to enter into my blood and hold me firm.

The two women paid a visit to the bungalow in the fall, "when we found the little house so silent under the pines, with the rich golden yellow of the pine needles on it and around it and a touch of the mellow autumn sunlight all about it." But now winter was coming, to both Arcady and Anne of Arcady.

Can't you see it in the wintertime, half buried under the snows, the sticks hanging from its eaves, the dead white forest keeping guard until life and laughter comes back in June. How the cold winds will howl down over the icebound lake!

99

When you are gone I'll feel like Arcady in the wintertime.
Ah, what a day it was of color and of sunshine . . . .

"There's one thing I won't ask you to remember, for I would never have you forget it in the first place, and that is that I love you," Mary wrote. "Your loyalty and truth have made me think well of the world sometimes, when I have been sorely tempted to think ill of it." Mary was happy for Anne. And while the connection "twixt thee and I" would endure, "soon in your heart must be a chamber that I may not enter—a holy of holies, kept for one alone. New hopes, new joys, new experience will be yours that I may not share."

Never for wealth, nor ease, nor the following of new paths, nor the sight of distant lands, nor the call of new adventures— tho these things are good. Not the protection of a strong arm, the companionship of a loyal heart, the love of a good man—tho these things are better.

There's a valley of the shadow thru which happy women pass—the bearing of a cross to be replaced by the crown of completed and perfected womanhood. If it should ever be your good fortune to some day hold in your arms your first-born, you will know why I envy you

Did you ever think, dear heart, that along this road lies immortality? . . . . The elixir of life that runs in our veins, that makes death seem so distant and unreal a thing, shall be our children's and our children's children's—an endless heritage.

Ah, this is best.

Tho I may dwell in Lonely Land
The memory of thy clasping hand
    Of many a joyous night and day
Is with me yet.

Goodbye, Goodbye, dear Heart
Thy path and mine must part.
    Thy footsteps on a flowery way
    Are firmly set.

For thee, the West, aglow
Beckons, and thou must go.
And though I would not bid thee stay
My eyes are wet.

Mary had a final poem to add. She entered "To Anne" into her journal on June 14, 1914—the day before Anne's wedding.

When tomorrow is today, love
Thy wedding day 'twill be.
All the little winds that blow
Up and down the wide world go
Seeking joy for thee.

It may be that the sun will shine
Full brightly on thy wedding day
It may be that the clouds will rise
And darken all the blue June skies
And hide the sun away.

What matters how the heavens lower
If in thy heart the sunlight bide
When every moment brings thee nearer
To the one who holds thee dearer.
Than all the world besides.

When tomorrow is today, love
Thy wedding day 'twill be.
All the little winds that blow
Up and down the wide world go
Bringing joy to thee.

A bungalow door also records Anne's transition from Arcady to Arkansas—and Mary's unintended role as matchmaker. Among the list of visitors in 1914 was "Mrs. Reed and Anne no longer Reed + Dick the reason therefore." Anne and her husband occasionally returned to Arcady. In one photograph, Dick stands with a toddler by his side next to the tent where Arcady's male visitors—the Gentle Knights that once included him—camped. In another photo, Anne and Mary pose stiffly together, unsmiling. Mary is taller than Anne, whose hand rests on Mary's shoulder. I found those negatives in a letter from Edmond, who likely took the pictures during a visit Mary cited in her journal. John Folsom was the son of Mary's brother Edwin. Janet Downs was Anne's daughter.

> August 27, 1915
> Ah the golden summer has gone again . . . . Two very new Arcadians were John Folsom and Janet Downs who are new on earth as well as in Arcady. They are nice babies. Anne and Dick came for an afternoon call and stayed from Tuesday until Friday owing to a broken axle. It is all I have seen or heard of Anne. Well, a baby is worth forgetting folks for. I'd forget if I could have one.

Even decades later, Mary clung to her times alone with Anne. In a June 12, 1935, letter to "Mrs. Ralph Downs," Mary recalled "the old days. They were surrounded by that light that glows not on land or sea—the joys that were."

Anne often returned to New Hampshire from Arkansas, especially for summers, to be closer to her mother and other family. After Ralph Downs died in 1943 at the age of fifty-seven, she moved back to the Granite State with her children, including her daughter Janet, the toddler in that photo. Anne visited Mary in both Epping and at Arcady, evidenced by a bungalow door inscription marking return of "Anne of Arcady" in 1953, this time with Janet and granddaughter Jeanette. That was more than four decades after Anne of Arcady first joined Mary at the lake. "Here's to the next 40 years," Mary scratched onto the door.

When she returned to Arcady nearly seventy years later, that granddaughter, Janet Downs White Jillette, did not recall that 1953 visit, when she was sixteen. But she remembered Mary and her grandmother Anne, whom she called Mimi. "Mimi was very special to me and her connection with Mary was very close and loving and long," Janet said as we sat on the bungalow porch in the fall of 2020. "Most of our relationships don't last very long but theirs lasted at least sixty years. Their strong ties from the past just continued like they had never been apart."

9. Sitting on Arcady's porch, Anne Reed's granddaughter, Janet Downs White Jillette, reads Mary's journal.

Arcady offered sanctuary to her grandmother, Anne Reed's granddaughter continued. "Mimi could be herself with Mary because when she lived in Arkansas, I don't think she could really be herself. She had to be more the wife of a cotton broker and she couldn't talk about her background or past life. For instance, she couldn't share with her Arkansas friends that her mother was an Irish immigrant, but she could tell May everything."

Anne Reed Downs died on October 15, 1970, in Wolfeboro, N.H. She was buried next to her husband at Graceland Cemetery in Pine Bluff, Ark.

Mary once mused about "coming back a hundred years or so to be one of those dim dancing creatures that [Anne and I] have half glympsed so many times." More than a century later, Anne's descendants and I could almost feel Mary and Anne sitting with us on the old porch, hearing the same lake ripple and watching the same tall pines shift in the wind. "Those two would make a very happy presence together," said Janet.

Chapter 9

In Skates "The Hero"

As she began the fourth book of her journals, Mary pondered "the blues" of her earlier passages.

> April 6, 1914
>
> There's always a little thrill when you begin a thing, and I like thrills. There's a little bit of wondering what will happen before the end is . . . . My poor third journal! It's a record of the blues mostly, of unhappy days and of unfulfilled desires of things that might have been but were not. I'm wondering what this will be. In the other when I wrote down a thing that I expected to do I was absolutely certain the thing wouldn't happen. It was strange magic, an uncanny charm. I hope it doesn't follow here, because I like to forecast my fate a bit without feeling that the forecasting forestalls.

The magic somehow faded. Mary neglected her journal for nearly a year. Maybe she was spent by the cathartic Idylls of Arcady that filled her previous volume. More likely, journaling became second fiddle to Mary's letter writing to "the Hero," Edmond G. Blair. From their first encounter in 1915 to their marriage in 1918, he and Mary often maintained a long-distance relationship and became loyal correspondents.

Mary was also dealing with work issues. Reliving the bad experience of her first teaching job in West Epping, Mary faced local resistance to how she interacted with her students, especially males, which conflicted with "the warped minds" of Hopedale officialdom. With soul mate Anne now gone to Arkansas, Mary turned to her journal, venting about small-town ways even as war raged across the sea.

> May 18th 1915. Peace Day
>
> I've just come from school where we have been singing the joys of Peace. They are vivid now in contrast with the bloody chaos into which Europe is plunged. I wonder when this awful slaughter will cease.
>
> I'm not particularly peaceful myself. I am so deathly sick of Hopedale. It is hell to me. All because people with crooked minds

insist on running things in crooked ways. That's all right. If they would hold their crooked tongues it would be all righter. First it is not seemly to go walking with boys in my class at school or in Sunday school—young enough to be my sons. Whether they corrupt my morals or I corrupt theirs I do not know, but at any rate, "People will talk." Even I must avoid impersonal conversation with any man for "People will talk." Burr! I am disgusted with the little warped minds of Hopedale folks.

That "Peace Day" heading indicated that Hopedale was one of many schools across the nation marking that annual commemoration, which began about a decade earlier when American isolationism prevailed. California Superintendent of Public Instruction Edward Hyatt explained Peace Day's purpose in 1915.

This is a particularly fitting time to emphasize and celebrate the idea of Peace. Our country is living in the midst of its manifold blessings, surrounded by the barbarities and sufferings that grim visaged War is inflicting upon the rest of the world. When Europe becomes exhausted with blood letting, it will be the duty and the privilege of our nation to lead in binding up the ragged wounds of war and in helping to restore the balance the war has upset. To serve that end it is highly desirable for us to preserve our own equilibrium now and to religiously avoid being drawn into the conflict or involved in its fierce heat in any way.

That isolationist intent probably appealed to Mary's Quaker soul. But her journal was more focused on far less global affairs, namely the new gentleman in her life. Mary was in fine spirits—she headed the entry, "Later—Some Saner"—as she wrote about her interest in Mr. Blair, despite her misgivings about the shape of his mouth, that ongoing Mary fixation. "H" referred to Hopedale; the meaning of "B.L." is unclear. Initially, Mary had no plans to pursue anything with Edmond.

There has been some excitement in H. too—just a little to relieve the monotony. Call it a drama with M.E. in the role of villainess.

It began last winter on the ice—Enter the hero. No—the
Hero—capital is misplaced. The Hero then labeled as the best
skater in Hopedale. One of my former pupils skated up to me
and announced that the Hero wished to be introduced. M.E.
was very absurdly flattered but when the lad fetched up the one
man in Hopedale that I had taken a very violent dislike to I felt
like pleading a sprained ankle. He was a man I had seen, never
been introduced, about every noon for a year, or so. He looks
immensely like [Mary's brother] Albert. I don't dislike him for
that reason. It's because every time I met him he seemed to be
tremendously amused by something in my appearance. I've gone
home and hunted for holes in my stocking or a smooch on my
nose or my petticoat longer than my dress, and I never could find
anything queerer than usual.

But after "skating with the man my prejudice began to evaporate."

The next time I skated with him it evaporated some more.
He offered to teach me the Dutch Roll. In the goodness of my
heart I told him he had better meet Miss Davis who is a most
excellent skater. Well, he met Miss Davis—enter heroine—and
I didn't learn the Dutch Roll . . . . I guess I might have had a
chance then, but no sir—With the perversity of the female
species, I started a B.L. myself and managed to make him
devote himself to me the rest of the evening.

Mary took "particular pains to skate as often as I could in the near
vicinity of the Hero," but expected nothing further to develop until,
the next day, "in pops Miss D. and sets the iron in me fair young soul by
relating how devoted the Hero had been."

Wouldn't that have jarred a saint? . . . . Next time there was
skating I just captured the Hero by fell strategy. He asked me to
skate about eight o'clock and I says, most amiably, "Well, I've
promised to skate with one of the Lyons girls, but if you want to

come round in half an hour or so"—What could he do? Why he couldn't skate with the Heroine, of course, for he skated with me 'til there wasn't any heroine left.

Then when I arranged a Valentine party, I'll admit I arranged it for the Hero to be detained while another man escorted the fair lady home. All—my villainy—since then it has been happenstance and I really haven't much prejudice left.

"The Hero," Mary continued, "is quite an interesting individual."

He is of French descent—hence his quickness to take a suggestion, I suppose. He seems to be a very devoted Roman Catholic—has an excellent vocabulary . . . . He is rather handsome —fair—but his mouth is too small. If it weren't for that I'd trust him implicitly—but, well I can't tell. 'Ware the small-mouthed person. I don't think Mr. Blair could be accused of that fault. He has a generous mouthful of white teeth and is remarkably good-natured. I'd like to see him mad just once—not with M.E., tho.

Edmond George Blair was born on December 3, 1888, in Burlington, Vt., making him about seven years younger than Mary. He was the youngest of three children of Jean Baptiste Blair and Alphonsine Dionne Blair. His ancestors were early settlers to Canada, coming to Quebec from France in the seventeenth century. The 1910 U.S. Census lists Edmond as a printer in Burlington. He held other jobs over the next decades, from metal worker and pattern maker to "wood heeler" for a shoe company to fireman in Hopedale, where he also played baseball. In his later years in Epping, he ran a printing shop and an insurance agency, both with mixed success.

Even as she pursued Edmond, Mary was interested in other men "in a fraternal sort of a fashion." Continuing her May 15, 1918, entry, Mary showed the gap between her "straight and narrow" public persona and how she really felt.

The day after—the night after—
The Island Party.

Did I say fraternal? I was mistaken. Nothing fraternal about it.
The mad moon of May, the fire light flickering down thru the
feathery pines. I've heard of duets and quartettes but never of
sextettes of lovers young dreams before. Fortunately it's only a
dream. Gee!! but it was some dream while it lasted. The Madness
of May is rather warping to those who plod along in the straight
and narrow way. And yet I'm wondering—which is warped—the
straight and narrow—or the other, which seems so infinitely more
right and natural. If a half a dozen men I know who've heard me
rail at all things aside from the straight and narrow ever heard
me admit that, wouldn't they set up one unholy shout of glee.
I suppose one really ought to investigate both sides before they
decide on the merits of either. I guess I'll investigate.

Declaring herself "unwarped" a few months later, Mary wrote that
she was going to teach and act as she saw fit, local reaction and authority
be damned. In this passage, Mary brought back up girlhood flame Will
Smith, whose alcoholism had become more apparent. (The "Keeley
Cure" was a mail order "secret" liquid formula that, while popular with
the general public, generated hostility within the medical establishment.).
Mary ended this entry with her evolving view of death as something not
dark, but possibly "desireable."

August 27, 1915
The golden summer has gone again. I have been so happy, so
very happy. I have been able to see clearly again and get my view
point a bit unwarped. Last year was an awful one. I cannot
understand the attitude of those whom I had thought my friends.
However I am going back to school and teach in my own way . . . .
Oh—if I could only get away from H. !!!
But this summer! It has been pure delight in camp and at home
. . . . Will Smith came over and called one evening . . . . I took him
out canoeing and the fog came up and while we drifted thru it

he told me all the things—no not all—but enough that he has done the last ten years. He says he has taken the Keeley Cure and reformed. It has been interesting to notice the results of alcohol on his brain. I used to think him quick-witted. He is still very fluent but he stammers and repeats and seems so much duller.

Poor boy. [His] fortunate mother asleep in peace, at rest in that sound-proof narrow chamber to which we all must come some day. Oh, blessed Heaven—Life, you've been pretty queer to me to let me think of that breathless darkness as a place desireable when it used to make me shudder and grow faint at heart.

Following this morose note, Mary neglected her journal for more than two-and-a-half years. But she had good cause for her inattention, she wrote on May 15, 1918. "Some lapse. That is because I've been so busy being in love with Edmond that I haven't had any time to write. I must write too. It would never do to leave too much space blank in my life record." Other major changes had come to Mary's life. After seventeen years of teaching in New Hampshire and Massachusetts, she decided to become a student again for the first time since finishing secondary school in 1900. In 1916, thirty-five-year-old Mary enrolled in Radcliffe College's "special student" program for older-than-college-age women. (See next chapter.).

After Radcliffe, Mary returned to teaching in Winthrop, Mass. Edmond had also left Hopedale in 1916 to work at the Navy Yard in Portsmouth, N.H., where he boarded in local hotels. During this period, the two saw each other mainly on weekends—their letters detailed train connection logistics—but they spent contented summers together at Arcady.

While that box I got from Edmond's niece contained only a few of Mary's letters to Edmond, it had hundreds from him to Mary, many of them page after fountain-penned page overflowing with adoration. "Wish you were here," he wrote on a Christmas 1915 postcard to Mary, who was spending the holidays back in West Epping. "Great skating and a dandy moon."

Early in their relationship, Edmond's letters were formal, addressed to "Miss Folsom" and signed with phrases such as "Cordially yours" and "Your sincere friend, Edmond G. Blair." Writing on February 6, 1915,

Edmond, referring to an article Mary had sent to him, was already aware that Mary Folsom was no typical female of the day. "I noticed your insert as to how to you were interested in the sharpening of skates," he wrote. "It must be that you are somewhat mechanically inclined to be interested in such. Because such things do not ordinarily interest the feminine mind, near as quick as the latest in spring hats and etc."

Edmond also recognized Mary's literary chops. "You certainly can write letters. I wish I could do about half as well, and then perhaps I would not find it quite so hard to answer. Youre descriptions of everything sound so much like yourself." Continuing that theme on July 29, 1915, Edmond wrote that "even under the best conditions, I am not very good [at writing]. However your beautiful long letter pleased me very much, even if I did have to pay two cents on it, you can write as many of them as you please and I shall gladly pay the extra postage."

This letter held an early reference to one of two challenges that emerged as the couple edged toward marriage. The first was religion. The other was looming war and the military draft. Edmond, a devout Catholic to Mary's Quaker, gently raised the religion issue, noting that one of her siblings had already wed a Catholic.

> So your brother went and married a catholic and you think she would meet with my approval . . . but she being a catholic would [not] make any difference with me. Most of the friends that I have had were not catholic . . . . When I like anybody I don't care what they are.
>
> Of course I know that mixed marriages are often times a bad thing, but I am certain that if two persons love each other that they will get along together without any trouble, and I hope that youre brother's case will be no exception to this rule.

Over time, Edmond became more open about his feelings. "My love for you goes back quite a way and I think that we both have been fooling ourselves into thinking that the feeling would not rise up in each-other," he wrote on July 10, 1916. "Dear, you and your kisses have meant more to me than you can imagine." Edmond exalted in his "new life of love" about three weeks later, likely after an Arcady weekend.

After I had washed off what looked like two tons of Boston & Maine RR soft coal . . . I lay in my bed and it seemed that my heart would break. I could see you in the doorway, and the expression on your face shall live in my memory forever . . . . Oh my dearest I wish I could think of some nice thing to say to you like those you say to me, but I can't express myself that way dear, but I do know that I love you as much as it's possible for anybody to love, and I am happy in this new life of love, happy because I have your love.

Youre great mind has taught me to see the right from the wrong, the mind that showed me how much more real pleasure there was to be had, in good companion-ship, than in the other, and made me see the enjoyment that could be found in the out door life, all these things dearest you have taught me . . . . You and I were made for each other and I feel that the just God will not be jealous of so much love.

God may have been fine with this relationship, but some folks on earth, especially members of Mary's family, were less than thrilled. In a letter to her mother, Mary defended Edmond and urged her parents to respect her judgment and her longing for a life partner. Mary wrote this letter shortly before Christmas, 1916. Just as the "Idylls of Arcady" was cathartic for Mary, so too was this intense letter, painful as it had to be to write. The context was that Edmond wanted to stay at the Folsom home in West Epping for a few days to await Mary's weekend arrival from Cambridge.

And will it be too much to ask of you and father to ask you to look upon him as kindly as you can. I think a great deal of him. The question of marrying him is one that is so far in the future that it may never materialize, but certainly I have never felt towards any man as I feel towards him. Every woman has a right to wish for a home and children of their own. Nothing in their world can fill those empty places in her heart. When you were my age your oldest daughter was nearly ten years old and your three boys were sturdy lads, and you had the love of a good man to depend on. Would you have been willing to exchange those things for a chance to earn your board and clothes and just a little more, and an old age free from actual want, but oh so much alone? I have feared it so much for myself—that being alone.

Mary knew her parents would have preferred a different mate, "but I am somewhat restricted in my chance to meet men," the letter continued.

Besides—if only I could feel your kindly interest in him I shouldn't care for any different choice. Outside of you and father, I have never known what it was to have anyone look out for me. I have been used to coming and going at all hours of the night in all sorts of weather, entirely dependent on myself. It has seemed good to me, for a year and a half, to know that someone had a thought of my comfort. I remember one stormy night last year. Mr. Blair met every car from half-past seven until eleven o'clock because he knew I had left town without an umbrella. Such thoughtfulness has been unwavering and it couldn't help but have some effect.

Mary wanted her parents to know some of what she found so special in Edmond.

I've never known him to lose his temper, tho I have been somewhat unmerciful at times with my propensity to tease. He has tried so hard to read the books I speak of, to enjoy the out-doors life that is so dear to me, to lay aside habits and companions that I have not liked, to understand and believe in my ideals. He is a Catholic, to be sure, but he is pretty broad-minded and I, at least, shall have to make no promises. He is younger than I—but that seems to run in the family.

As I said before, the prospect of marrying the man is very far in the future. I should want to be absolutely sure of both his feelings and mine, and sure of his ability to take care of me, tho I haven't much doubt of that.

Please give him as cordial a welcome as you can find it in your hearts to do, and if your feeling against him is so strong, remember that he has always shown me every possible courtesy and consideration.

Aware of broader familial unhappiness with the relationship, Mary suggested that her mother downplay Edmond's visit to the family of Mary's brother Edwin, who lived next door. "Don't feel fussed over Blair. We can store him away in the little room, or somewhere. The people in the other house need only know that he has a holiday Monday and that if it is good skating and snow-shoeing we are looking forward to enjoying it."

Other Folsom family members were at best ambivalent about Mary's choice of this younger French-Canadian Catholic man, including Fred Perry, the son of Mary's late sister Mabel. Fred, who was enrolled at the Naval Academy at Annapolis, Md., invited his Aunt Mary to be his guest at the Army-Navy football game. He hoped she'd be married by then, but not to a member of "the heathen set."

> November 13, 1916
> I imagine and hope that I shall write Mrs. Mary Evelin _____ and not Miss Mary Evelin Folsom to see the Navy trim the Army in 1917. . . . I read your letter with great interest when I read about the <u>man</u>. But don't tell me he belongs to that heathen set!! If he does—you know what I think of him. ((I hope I'm not treading on forbidden ground, or disturbing the peace of a heart that has at last found its affinity)).

For his part, neither religion nor distance deterred Edmond. Just a week after receiving Fred's anti-Catholic admonition, Mary got another love letter from Edmond on November 20, 1916. "As I lay in bed last night I would have given most anything to kiss your lips tonight as I did a week ago this night, but my dear next Sunday we will be together. Good night my dear. I love you, I love you."

Besides religion, the other major cloud over their relationship was their fear that Edmond could be conscripted for the expanding war in

Europe. Initially, Edmond seemed less troubled by the winds of war. "My dear, I hardly think that they will pass the draft bill, and I think the war will be over before summer comes, this same question is bothering quite a few around here," he wrote in early 1917. As fellow townsmen marched off to service, Edmond was torn between patriotic duty and his love of Mary.

> April 12, 1917
> Yesterday was quite a day . . . . The Co M boys left for Springfield there were many sad sights to be sure. I felt very funny as the train pulled out of the station. I shall never forget it. It was not because I thought of the actual horror of actual combat, the bursting of shrapnell.
> The fumes of poisonous gas, the deadly curtain of fire or the dreadful liquid fire. These things dearest would not bother me but the thought of leaving you would be more dreadful to me than any other thing. It made my legs shake under me and caused a lump in my throat that I couldn't easily swallow. My dear I pray that this awful thing that is going on will come to an end and that peace shall again be restored and save many young lives and broken hearts.

As part of the Army's Boston-based 26th Infantry Division, also known as the Yankee Division, Company M saw heavy combat in France during World War I. Young men, many of them rural and with little training, found themselves in the muddy hell of trench warfare. From when the United States declared war on Germany on April 6, 1917, until the Armistice that ended it on November 11, 1918, more than a million American military personnel were deployed in Europe. About 53,400 died from battle wounds and another 63,000-plus died from influenza and other non-combat causes. A plaque at the State Capitol in Concord lists 697 New Hampshire men and women who died during "The Great War."

Edmond did not want Mary to think he was unwilling to join the war effort.

May 1, 1917

Oh my dear what a dreadful thing it is to look forward to being taken from you. I try dear not to think of such a thing happening but oh my dearest one I sometimes fear that it shall come. My dear perhaps you may think that I am not loyal to my country but my dear love of country and love of you are not to be compared. If I didn't have you to live for, I would be off tomorrow to the nearest recruiting station to answer the call . . . [but] how could I bear to leave you. You are my share of this world, also my share of Heaven, and to have to leave you now not knowing when to see you again, Why! The very sun would drop out of my Heaven.

Devotion to Mary prevailed over the recruiting office; Edmond wrote on June 6, 1917, that he had found a way to avoid being called up. "I registered [for the draft] this afternoon. I put down that I had a widower mother partially dependent, that I was a fireman, also that I was a metal pattern maker and a machinist, now all we can do is to await my fate. I have a feeling my dear that I shall not be drafted, however it [is] a chance."

Months later, Mary remained worried.

September 3, 1917

My dearest one . . .

I have missed you so. Last night I had to go out to the shed several times for wood, and the bright moonlight made me think of you. Most everything makes me think of you . . . . I have thought of the farewell at Exeter and the one kiss I didn't give you of all the kisses since that first one that you took. I missed it all the way home and ever since, and I reckon I'll have to give it with interest the next time we meet.

I have felt an unease of mind since Arcady. It is a fear that something will prevent our final union. Our love has been wonderfully perfect. Perhaps it is a relic of the old pagan superstition that the gods are jealous of the perfect happiness and good fortune of mortals and send trouble to even it up. I don't know anything more tangible than the fear that a year or two from now will find you "somewhere in France." I saw a soldier saying goodbye to a circle of weeping women the other day. They clung to him and he was very frankly crying, too. God pity us if we say "Goodbye" so . . . .

I love you—more than ever I believe.

Your Mary

To further reduce the risk of conscription, Edmond had his job at the Portsmouth, N.H., Navy Yard as a metal worker and pattern maker. This would likely protect him "as long as the war lasts and possibly for sometime afterwards," he wrote on January 20, 1918. "Just as long as I am allowed to stay here, and it keeps me from leaving you, we have lots to be thankful for."

Edmond's focus was now squarely on turning Mary Folsom into Mrs. Edmond Blair. "God knows that if such a thing as getting married to-morrow was possible, I would be the happiest man in this world to-night. My dear what will be my state when our wedding day comes," read a June 25, 1917, letter. "I just shut my eyes so that nothing can distract my mind from that one thing and picture us coming down the center isle, after those sacred words have been said, that shall bind us so close to each other dear that only in death will we part."

But who would marry them and where? Edmond wanted a Catholic priest to perform the ceremony in a Catholic Church. Mary was willing to go along, albeit probably not enthusiastically, which might explain why Mary wanted to keep the likelihood of marriage to Edmond under wraps. Edmond updated Mary of his wedding machinations, which included finding a priest willing to marry this mixed-religion couple.

November 15, 1917

Last night I called on Father Dunphy and told him my story. He was very much interested and said if it were not for the fact that I perhaps would have to have a license from Hopedale that we could be married just as quietly right in Milford as we could any place and he said that he could fix it up with the town clerk in Milford so that it would not go on the records of Milford but of course would go on the state records, which would not be anything because nobody would ever take the pains to look up the matter here . . . . I have not the least doubt my dear but that we can pull it off.

Edmond reported further progress—and secrecy—four days later. "You will be interested to know that the good father told me that . . . the only trouble would be keeping it out of the papers, which he said would be a very easy matter. He said that he knew both of the reporters very well, and that he could fix that part of it."

A small, almost clandestine Catholic ceremony was not the kind of wedding Mary had envisioned, Edmond admitted.

> December 10, 1917
> Oh dearest love how I wish it was possible for me to give you a very formal wedding. I realize my dear just what this event means to most girls, and if it were possible we would have it, but as you say the future has so many uncertainties that if we are to give ourself to each other, it must be this way. Oh dearest one if we can't have a pretty wedding like many that have such weddings and nothing else, not even a mutual love for each other. We can at least have our simple ceremony, and be just as much wedded as any to persons could be and my dear if an eternal love can make us happy under these conditions we should ask for no more.

Edmond's initial plans with the local priest fell apart, but he said he would find another priest to marry them. He knew he was trying Mary's patience, as he wrote in early 1918 (the letter's postmark is illegible.).

> My dear love these obstacles that fate has seen fit to put in our way has only served to make me love you all the more . . . .
> However my dear I hope that very soon that I shall have the chance of letting [the first priest] know that in spite of his unwillingness to marry us, that we had succeeded in finding a father that was willing to let down the bars [for] two persons that dearly love each other . . . .
> My dear, this latter trouble makes me fully realize how far you are going to meet me, and I know that what is asked of you

is considerable. But dearest one these things I know can be very easily adjusted between you and I after all other things have had their course.

Using stationery from Portsmouth's Hotel DeWitt, where he was probably boarding, Edmond wrote Mary on February 18, 1918, that he was anxious for "that time comes when we . . . can have together the hours of companionable sweetness as one." He reassured her that "I shall see what can be done towards keeping our wedding quiet for a while at least." On April 9, 1918, ten days before the wedding, Edmond wrote to ask Mary when she would arrive in Portsmouth. "Oh my dear how happy I shall be when this engaging of rooms for you shall not be necessary, when I can have you by my side the whole night long."

At long last, their wedding day arrived on April 19, 1918.

As Mary would later note in the letter to Anne's mother cited in Chapter 7, the wedding was a small affair, with only a handful of Edmond's friends and family and none of Mary's in attendance. According to their wedding certificate, the ceremony was performed by Father John P. Moran, assistant pastor of the Church of the Immaculate Conception in Portsmouth. Mary was thirty-five, Edmond twenty-nine. "After a wedding breakfast at the Rockingham House Mr. and Mrs. Blair went by automobile to Mrs. Blair's camp 'Arcady' at the Pawtuckaway Lake, where they spent the weekend," according to a local newspaper notice.

Two days after the wedding, with Mary back in her Massachusetts classroom, Edmond addressed a letter with the salutation he had long pined to use. "My dearest wife. I'm just as proud of being your husband as you are in being my wife . . . . We have been uplifted to where serene love blends into perfect harmony. A place where not one single flower in our garden of love shall ever perish. Oh my dear how wonderful it all is."

"We are very happy in each other."

It took her two years to get around to it, but Mary finally recounted her wedding day in her journal. "It isn't reasonable to leave so many blank spaces in the record—but years and years slip by," she began.

October 10, 1920

When I [last wrote] in 1918 I was within a few weeks of my wedding day. Edmond and I were married the 19th of April—1918. We felt that any day he might be sent overseas and it seemed impossible to think of a possible separation that might be permanent, before we had taken those vows that made as one in the eyes of God and man. We were already one spiritually, for we had come to know and love each other very dearly.

My wedding day was gloriously beautiful, clear blue sky with white clouds and a good wind blowing. We were married at Portsmouth by the assistant rector of the Catholic church. Only Florence and a friend of Edmond's and Sam Ladd, then mayor of Portsmouth, were present. We had a wedding breakfast at the Rockingham. Then Uncle Ed Smith met us and drove us up to camp. No place like Arcady for our honeymoon. I think it sort of welcomed us for when I waited just beyond the gate for Edmond to bring along some things, I looked down at my feet and there were my own name-flowers, may flowers, pink and white, coy brides of the spring breezes and sunshine, blushing me a welcome.

We busied ourselves cleaning up the camp and twilight came down, soft and purple, no glaring colors, but all misty harmonies. We kindled the fire upon the hearth and the night grew black outside and shut the world away from us—And the wind was in the trees—And the fire died down.

Next day we went mayflowering and found such sweet beauties. That night it rained and we listened to the rain on the roof and felt happy in the peace and seclusion.

The couple returned to their jobs, Edmond to Portsmouth and Mary to Massachusetts. On weekends, the couple "renewed our honeymoon . . . . There was heaven in the weekends. Edmond was not called at all, but I lived so much in fear of his going. Armistice day was a happy one for me. We are very happy in each other."

10: This undated photo may be Mary Folsom and Edmond Blair on their wedding day.

One of Arcady's walls also records their wedding; the writing on the dark wood has faded over more than a century, but not the message: "1918. Edmond and I, April 18-20—A happy year!"

For all her new-found happiness, Mary returned to an old lament. "There have been no children. I am so afraid there never will be." Mary felt the passage of time, especially as she continued to lose close relatives, including her brother and a nephew, though she ended this catch-up entry on a brighter note.

> There are so many empty spaces in our lives now. Mother
> sits near me tonight, but father's chair has been empty three years
> in January. I miss him so. Last December—after a desperate fight
> against tuberculosis—Albert went very suddenly. Tom was taken
> sick two weeks later and died the 30th of March—a dear good
> boy, full of high ideals and honest and upright. They are all at rest
> in the little Quaker graveyard where so many of our people lie.

This afternoon Edmond and I went up on the intervale and picked cranberries. There were a lot of them. There was a gorgeous sunset and Edmond and I walked home in the twilight, happy at our success. Mother we fooled by putting pine cones on the top of the basket and a long face on ourselves. She was properly surprised when the pine cones were removed.

Strange, is it not, that life is made up of so many very simple little things that spell the deepest content if they are only shared with the one we love.

Part Three

Outside Schoolhouse Walls

Chapter 10: To Radcliffe—and back to Epping

After teaching Grade 8 at the Dutcher Street School in Hopedale from 1911 to 1915, Mary worked in Winthrop, Mass. After one year, she took leave from her classroom to become a full-time "special student" at Radcliffe College. It is unclear how or when Mary learned about Radcliffe, though it may have been from a Foxboro acquaintance who had attended the school. Mary wrote nothing in her journals about her year in Cambridge. Perhaps classes kept her too busy to write anything other than school work. Perhaps she kept a separate Radcliffe year diary that was lost when her house was emptied.

Mary also lagged in her letters to Edmond, who gently reprimanded her. "Only one letter from you last week," he wrote on October 1, 1916. "I realize dear that you have plenty of work cut out for yourself in doing your college work . . . . As much as I enjoy you're letters, I willingly sacrifice that joy for your own welfare."

That welfare meant going to Cambridge, not that Harvard University wanted female students through its crimson gates. Harvard President Charles William Eliot made the university's official view clear in his 1869 inaugural address. "The world knows next to nothing about the natural mental capacities of the female sex. Only after generations of civil freedom and social equality will it be possible to obtain the data necessary for an adequate discussion of women's natural tendencies, tastes, and capabilities."

Ten years later, persistent advocacy by the Woman's Education Association of Boston led to the creation of a program for the "Private Collegiate Instruction for Women" in 1879, in which a few Harvard professors agreed to repeat their lectures to groups of private female students. Though it had no formal relationship with the university, the program became known as the "Harvard Annex." In 1894, the Commonwealth of Massachusetts approved the establishment of Radcliffe College, though Harvard remained all-male. (Radcliffe was not fully incorporated into the university until 1999.). Indeed, just months after Radcliffe's founding, the Harvard Board of Overseers adopted a resolution that the Bachelor of Arts degree not be given to women by the university under any circumstances.

Rather than earning a formal college degree, "special students" such as Mary "were at college to deepen their knowledge of a particular field," according to *A Century to Celebrate: Radcliffe College, 1879-1979*. "Usually they were, or intended to be, teachers of that subject in college preparatory schools." The special students, most of whom spent one year at Radcliffe, often came from Greater Boston. "The present policy of the College admits as special students none but the mature; and among the mature who are eager and qualified for academic work teachers are naturally numerous," noted Harvard's 1917 *Annual Report to Radcliffe College*. With fifteen years in a classroom, Mary fit that profile.

Of 697 students enrolled at Radcliffe for the 1916-1917 academic year, seventy-one were special students, according to the report. "Of these, 18 teachers were admitted under the arrangement with a few public schools by which, in return for an opportunity given Radcliffe students to teach in these schools, a certain number of teachers are given free instruction in Radcliffe College each year." Though a Massachusetts teacher, Mary did not merit free tuition, as indicated in her correspondence with school officials.

In her application, which I found in the archives of the Schlesinger Library on the History of Women in America at the Radcliffe Institute for Advanced Study (where Mary's papers will reside), Mary listed eight courses she wanted to take during her Radcliffe year: English Literature; Contemporary Literature; English Composition; European History; The American Nation; Play in Education; Methods of Teaching; and Psychology.

That was one half course too many, Radcliffe officials told her. Mary appealed for the extra course. "I am sorry to say the ruling of the Chairman is that the rule which has been made, must hold for all special students admitted after 1915," said Radcliffe's October 3, 1916, letter in response. "That is, a special student cannot take more than four courses" per semester. True to form, Mary was not deterred. She appealed again on February 12, 1917, offering a pointed lesson on basic arithmetic to the Cambridge pooh-bahs.

> In the spring of 1916 my attention was called to the courses offered at Radcliffe to the student seeking to enter as a special . . . .
> I received from the office a copy of the Radcliffe 1916 catalogue.

On page 43 of that catalogue is a paragraph that seems to offer liberal opportunity to specials. On the strength of it, I gave up a remunerative position and made arrangements to enter Radcliffe in the fall. When I registered last September I was informed that by a very recent ruling, no special student was to be allowed to take more than four courses.

For the fall semester, I signed for the following courses: Eng 41 2) Eng 31 3) Hist 1 4) Ed 10 5) Ed 12a

The first three are full courses extending throughout the year. Ed 10 is a half course, one period a week. Ed 12a was a half course, ending at midyear. When I applied . . . for permission to take Ed 12b the second semester, I was refused on the grounds that I already had my four courses. According to my system of mathematics, the cessation of Ed 12a leaves me with only three and a half courses.

That left Mary "with much extra time on my hands the first half year and I feel that more time is most undesirable. I pay the same tuition that you receive from students to whom you give the privilege of five courses."

I have been a teacher in your Massachusetts schools for the past ten years. Both my years and my mind may be considered mature. I have made definite sacrifices in order to acquire this more liberal education and I have done it with a special object in view . . . . I cannot believe that it is the policy of Radcliffe to deliberately discourage the earnest worker. I ask the careful consideration of my request.

Radcliffe relented four days later, permitting Mary to take her full course load. She graduated from the Radcliffe program in 1917, earning mostly "Bs" in her classes.

While at Radcliffe, Mary lived at 11 Arlington Street in Cambridge, which was the home of Meta Robitscheck Rothschild, the widow of Alonzo Rothschild, who drowned near his home in Foxboro in 1915, when he was fifty-four. A Harvard graduate, Alonzo founded *Jeweler's*

Weekly in 1885, the success of which enabled him to retire and become an independent Lincoln scholar and author of *Lincoln: Master of Men* and *Honest Abe*.

Alonzo, Meta, and their children lived in Foxboro while Mary was teaching there, so she may have taught one or more of the children, two of whom were grade schoolers at the time. Meta also "took special courses at Radcliffe," according to an unpublished biography of Alonzo written by his son John Rothschild. However it began, the Rothschild-Mary relationship lasted well beyond that year in Cambridge. "Rothschild" appeared on the walls of Arcady several times, beginning in 1923. A September 14, 1939, door etching listed "Hon. Meta Rothschild, Selectman, Foxboro" and her children.

After Radcliffe, Mary spent the summer of 1917 at Arcady with her usual stream of visitors, especially Edmond. During the subsequent school year, Mary lived in a Massachusetts boarding house during the week but regularly returned to West Epping. After her seventy-seven-year-old father died on January 3, 1918, Mary spent more time with her mother, who was increasingly unable to keep up with the house and small farm.

Mary sought further education through that era's version of continuing education, likely by correspondence, at the State Normal School in North Adams, Mass. But demands at home caused her to fall behind on some of her assignments, as Mary explained in a January 8, 1918, letter to Hannah P. Waterman, who supervised the training of sixth grade teachers at the Normal School. Mary did not want her "to think the neglect due to carelessness."

> Mother and I are alone on the farm this winter, and we are taking care of eight and sometimes nine head of cattle besides a horse and some hens. I help about this work morning and night, also bring in the wood, besides driving to school which is three miles away. Of course I have my school work to prepare also. As you will see, this keeps me very busy and it is especially hard as we have never before done any work out of doors.
>
> I managed very nicely with the work and prepared my lessons in the evening usually between nine and half past eleven or twelve, until that heavy snow storm when I had to shovel snow to get

to the barn and hen house, and so many extra things to do that I was too tired to work on my discussions. Then this cold spell has made it very hard too, so until last evening I could not stay up at night to work on my lessons. But now that it is warmer again it will be easier and I hope to get rested and I can make up any time I may have lost and continue on the lessons, as I am very anxious to finish the course.

Mary ended on more positive notes. "The school committee have bought a book of Mother Goose Rhymes for my use. Since I sent in the lesson Dramatization we have dramatized A Stone in the Road and The Wolf and the Crane . . . . I was very much pleased and encouraged to receive the A mark in connection with my tenth lesson."

Replying on February 6, 1918, Waterman urged Mary to keep plugging. "Like so many other things we postpone, the effort is worth while if we can only make it, is it not!"

At some point that year, likely after Mary finished teaching, Edmond and Mary moved into the Folsom home in West Epping, where the two spent the rest of their lives. She was now Mary Evelyn Folsom Blair. For the rest of her life, Mary was back in her small rural hometown.

This Mary was a far more experienced educator than the fresh Sanborn Seminary graduate who was so frustrated by her first teaching job in 1901 that she fled West Epping to work elsewhere for a decade-and-a-half. In her first year back at Epping in 1918, Mary was one of three teachers overseeing thirty-four grade school students. Classes barely began when they were halted. "From Sept. 27 to Oct. 21 no school on account of epidemic" Mary wrote into the official Epping school register. That epidemic was the Spanish Flu of 1918-1919.

The second wave of an H1N1 virus that had been coursing through Europe and the United States for months, that flu killed millions across the world, including an estimated 675,000 Americans and more than 2,500 people in New Hampshire, over just four months. Though some major cities, including Chicago and New York, kept their classrooms open, schools across the nation closed for weeks to months. After all, the U.S. Bureau of Education declared in 1916 that the "education of the schools is important, but life and health are more important." But with alternatives such as remote learning unimaginable, some localities, especially rural and economically struggling ones such as Epping, resisted extensive closures.

The flu wasn't the only disruption facing Mary during this period. "The school was closed in October because there was no stove," Mary E. F. Blair wrote in the 1919 school register. "Three weeks were lost. It was closed again in January and February because the second hand stove in use was not adequate for the purpose. Five weeks were lost. We have made up about half the time by teaching from February 23 to July 9 without formal vacation."

In the fall of 1920, Mary was back in the West Epping Rural School a half-mile down the road from the home in which she grew up and now lived with her husband and mother. The nineteenth-century schoolhouse originally had just one room; a second was added in 1923 to accommodate more students. The wood frame building had a kitchen, wood shed, and bathrooms and was just around the corner from the West Epping Quaker Meeting house.

Mary, who grew up with the parents of some of the children she was now teaching, was attuned to how her charges were faring outside of school as well as inside. In the 1920s, West Epping was a rural village, with many families struggling. She made both her school and her own home social service centers of sorts, reflecting her determination to blend the classroom and outside worlds. Mary's attendance log for 1920-1921 was a snapshot of the era. Reasons for student absences included: "Mother sick." "No Rubbers" "No Clean Clothes" "Chicken Pox" "Fear of Contagion." In 1923, Violet Clement and Lila Denyou missed classes because of Whooping Cough; Emma Martin was out for a few days "watching cows." The next school year saw a "low percentage of attendance due to a winter of severe colds, influenza and pneumonia."

Parents appreciated Mary's attentiveness to their children's needs in and out of the school house. "I wish to thank you for the care and kindness you have shown the children," M. J. Westcott wrote in a note to Mary. "They have both learned to respect and love you dearly."

Former students remember

Decades after they left her school, former students recalled how Mary's aid and comfort helped offset hardships at home and in the broader community. I reached out to some of them in the 1990s, when many of them were nearing or in their eighties. One of them, Jennie True, lived just a few houses away from the school. "I completely remember that school during the Depression years," Mrs. True, who was born in 1914, told me. "After one Christmas vacation, Mrs. Blair and the teacher who taught in the next room saw how thin and white the children looked. Times were so hard that my father couldn't even find a job cutting cord wood. I remember the teachers went into the kitchenette between the two rooms and cried."

Like other former students, she recalled how Mary assigned them not just homework, but responsibilities. "I used to help with the hot lunches," she said. "Sometimes I'd cook about four pounds of macaroni before noon. I think she bought the food out of her own pocket. We made what she called Mulligan stew—someone would bring a can of carrots, someone something else—she'd put it all together." Regular fare included chowder, stew, and cocoa for students who could not go home for lunch.

Just as Mary's long, unchaperoned hikes through the forest would likely be frowned upon today, so too would this Quaker's willingness to strap the misbehaving wrist. "She was very stern," said one of my Epping neighbors. "When she got mad, you'd know it. Her face would turn red and she'd come right at you and even take you into the woodshed with her strap." Ryan Willey, who was in Mary's classroom as she neared retirement in the 1950s, recalled that she also turned to "a size 15 slipper" as a behavioral remedy. "She was tough, but she was a great teacher," said Willey, who regularly visited Mary on trips home to Epping during his long Air Force career.

Ramona Stevens graduated Mary's eighth grade in 1934, a few years after Jennie True. "Mrs. Blair taught by having the children do, not just with books or with penmanship, but with good work experiences." Mary launched an informal hot lunch program, long before such efforts became systemic. "Each student was given a designated time for their turn to prepare the meal," recalled Ramona.

11. Mary rings the West Epping Rural School bell.

Pushing the age of eighty, Leonard "Bud" Purington was still running his one-man sawmill a few miles from Epping when he and I spoke. "Mrs. Blair made sure none of us went hungry," he said. She also made sure things were all right at home. "If one of the kids was in trouble, she'd have him come to her house after school and after dinner, she'd go over the things that were bothering him."

One of Bud's chores was to haul firewood to the school from Mary's land a half-mile from the school. As Bud explained that task, I recognized certain landmarks he described, like a sharp bend along the narrow dirt road—aptly named Old Cart Path—that runs from the highway and past my little house to the river. How long since you've been down that road? I asked. "Oh, fifty years or so," Bud replied. Days later, I drove him down that same dirt road into the forest that he had so precariously traversed with loads of firewood. "I was always afraid that the wagon was going to top over, with me in it," he said, chuckling at the old memory.

Like many in West Epping, Bud had siblings and other relatives who also studied under Mary, who taught three generations of some families. That included the Trues—Jennie True's son Forrest graduated Mary's eighth grade in 1949. Forrest was one of two student janitors, with tasks ranging from stoking the stove to fetching water when the school pump failed. "I'd start the fire at five or six a.m. so that the stoves were red hot by the time the teachers got there," said Forrest. He too cited Mary's compassion and generosity. "My mother was one of twelve siblings and many times, they had nothing and Mrs. Blair bought clothes for them. The town paid us a little money but she would give us more." Over time, Mary expanded her social service role, even helping to launch a local dental clinic that was available to all students, regardless of financial status.

Forrest, whose great grandfather Enoch True built the West Epping Friends Meeting House, agreed that Quaker Mary also had a tougher edge, especially when it came to the older students in her age-mixed classroom.

"Every morning, we would say the Lord's Prayer," he said as we spoke in the wood-frame building in the town center that is home to the Epping Historical Society, where Forrest's wife Joy and other volunteers spend countless hours trying to preserve the legacy of their nearly three-century-old town. "We had to put our heads down on our desks for ten minutes. Once, on my birthday, I didn't. She came right over to me. 'Mr. True, just because it's your birthday doesn't mean you need not put your head down.' If you really misbehaved, you'd get your knuckles whacked. She'd also punish kids by putting them under her desk. But you didn't get punished unless you deserved it."

In 1967, Virginia Willey—Ryan's mother—profiled the former teacher for *New Hampshire Profiles* magazine, starting with how Mary took troubled youngsters into her home.

She would fill the round brass bed warmer with red coals, go to the upper guest chamber, heat the feather bed thoroughly and tuck the youngster in under homespun blankets woven by her Quaker ancestors 100 years ago.

Mrs. Blair read all things which she considered beautiful and inspirational. The lovely songs and psalms of the Bible, Dickens, Tennyson, Longfellow, Robert Frost and historical books full of adventure and daring. She read "Hiawatha" and the rhythm and beauty of her voice carried the classroom along on a river of lovely sound.

Willey's article made clear how Mary was ahead of her educational times.

In Mrs. Blair's room there were no set rules of education. Pupils were allowed to talk with one another and if one was slow in a subject another student who was especially good tutored him along . . . . Each pupil was permitted to use his own judgment and because Mrs. Blair trusted her students there was no cheating. They learned because she made them know they wanted to. If a child became defiant or stubborn, Mrs. Blair took him for one of her well known walks. Nobody liked this parade around the classroom in front of all the others, and one promenade left no desire for a repeat performance . . . .

Many girls and boys stood erect and proud on graduation day because she knew what size dress they wore or what size shoe to buy; others received diplomas because she spent hours tutoring them. No child was ever the butt of amusement in Mrs. Blair's school and none was ridiculed because of his clothes or home, color, or religion. Ties with Mrs. Blair were not severed at school's end. Her hand of friendship is always outstretched to those who need it.

Robert Tuttle, who went on to become Dean of the University of Texas Medical School, credited Mary for his success. "What she represented and what she did had real meaning for people who lived in this town," he said as we taped the *Chronicle* episode in 2000.

12. Mary with one of her classes.

Former students also recalled the plays Mary wrote and produced for holidays and other occasions. During "Education Week" in 1923, according to one of Mary's school registers, "the pupils gave a dramatization of Rip Van Winkle attended by about sixty parents and friends, who took this opportunity of showing their interest in the school." In 1928, "At the Christmas exercises, over 150 guests were present."

Mary Folsom Blair's productions became town-wide events. In 1941, the bi-centennial pageant she wrote and directed with a cast of 175 local people drew 4,500 spectators to the Hedding Campground in Epping. Entertaining and educational, the plays enabled Mary's students to be teachers within their own community. Using dialogue that quoted Plato, the Magna Carta, and the classics, Mary's grade schoolers displayed the

13. Mary in her West Epping classroom, 1940s.

depth of their learning in this small rural school. An example is the West Epping Grammar School's 1943 Lincoln's Day play. Mary's hand-written script moved swiftly through Lincoln's life, with some details that my own public education somehow missed. After describing his log cabin years, student narrators moved to Lincoln's later life.

> Nancy
> While he studied law, he had to eat. So he split rails and kept a store. And he earned his living any honest way. Once he helped to take a raft down the Mississippi to New Orleans. There he saw black folks sold at auction.

> Vivian
> Yes, there he saw slaves sold. Saw men and women sold like dumb cattle. But when babies were taken from their mothers

arms—When husbands and wives were separated—It was not like
dumb cattle. "I will do what I can" said young Abraham Lincoln
"To stamp out this evil."

Norma
What could he do? This boy from the wilderness. This six feet
of muscle and of strength. This homely and awkward scrawny
lad. Poor, no rich friends, no powerful helpers. What could
he do?

The script went through Lincoln's political career, presidency, the
January 1, 1863, Emancipation Proclamation ("What a New Year for
a million slaves"), the Civil War, and the "with malice toward none"
eloquence of his Second Inaugural. Mary must have been uncertain how
to end her play, based on the script's final line: "On April 14th 1865 he
was (murdered) assassinated," read the multiple choice ending.

The eighth graders in that same 1943 class held a graduation
exercise that, according to the narrator, "is not very long but it means
a lot to us. It means that for eight years more or less we have spent
gaining tools with which to work. We have the freedom to make a
choice of what comes next. We may not get just what you choose but
we can at least try." Mrs. Blair, read the script—written, of course, by
Mrs. Blair herself—"said that she had spent four years in educating
us until the edges of her tongue were nearly worn off."
All that tongue lashing led to some global recognition, explained the
narrator in the play that Mary wrote for her school's 1945 graduation.

Two years ago we wrote a Thanksgiving play in this room,
as we do every Thanksgiving. At that time, a friend of Mrs. Blair's
was working in Washington with the O.W.I [the Office of War
Information]. English people all over the world were interested
in American things and the O.W.I. asked for samples of work in
American schools. Mrs. Blair was asked to send some of her plays,
which she did. They went to Australia, South Africa, India, and
England. The English people liked the Thanksgiving play so well

that the British Broadcasting Company sent an agent to West Epping to get a record of the play.

She drilled us 2 days, picking out the children whose voices she thought would record well. Then we went to Manchester to WMUR, drilled some more, and made the record.

The BBC could not locate any records of that recording.

Chapter 11

Getting young people outdoors

If former students had warm recollections of their times inside Mary's schoolhouse, their memories of their times outside of it were even more vivid. Long before it was so labeled, Mary embraced the classroom-without-walls concept. Though many of her rural town students were often outside for cow milking and other chores, Mary wanted them to more completely appreciate the natural world. "All of Mary's students grew up with not only an education, but with a better understanding of nature," said her great-nephew, Neal Folsom.

That outdoor emphasis resonated with me. In the late 1950s and early 1960s, Jennie Anderson, who was my father's second grade teacher in the 1920s, was my boyhood baby-sitter. Her approach to child tending included sending me into the woods with my dog Caesar to look for frogs or to catch butterflies. Short and very un-athletic, I was able to find self-confidence in the woods. At summer camp, I may have been the last kid picked for the softball team, but bunkmates knew to turn to me to trap the chipmunk they needed for the annual scavenger hunt. I'd have thrived in Mary's teaching world.

She wanted everyone, especially her students, to savor nature as much as she reveled in describing it. "Though I am a native of New Hampshire, I have never seen my own granite hills," she wrote in her journal on July 28, 1913, after a trip to the White Mountains. Riding the cog railway through and up Crawford Notch, she wrote, "I looked down the steep sides to the tops of the great trees so many hundreds of feet below. I found myself clutching the side of the train and holding it on to the mountain by my eyelid. How have they got along without M.E. all these years."

In verse-like prose, she described the evening view from her lodging in Bretton Woods, near Mount Washington.

> I watched Night come over the mountain. Wonderful grey mists setting down shutting the sky-piercing peak from view— slowly descending till they reached the level of my eyes—then I looked in the valley and black night was there made blacker by

twinkling lights. I have a vision of Night—would I could paint it—a woman of titanic stature touches one bare foot to the mountain top—alighting from cloudy chariot—she bends with outstretched hands toward the weary earth—from her limbs float misty trailing garments—her black hair flying wild form blue-black clouds on either side—her brows are level and madonna like—for night gives rest and peace—to her tired little people—but her mouth is scarlet—a drooping bow—emblem of the passion that blossoms—flower of the night—and scarlet poppies crown her head.

Mary's determination to get others, especially the young, to similarly absorb the natural world extended well beyond the classroom. In Massachusetts, she became involved with Camp Fire Girls, which was founded in 1910 by Luther and Charlotte Vetter Gulick, who "believed girls deserved the outdoor learning experiences that boys had and wanted to help 'guide young people on their journey to self-discovery.'" Camp Fire girls received outdoor education and skills, often donning Native American garb during ceremonial activities. (Camp Fire Girls became just "Camp Fire" after the admission of boys in 1975.).

Camp Fire and similar efforts reflected the strength of the "nature study movement" of the late nineteenth and early twentieth century. Direct contact with the outdoors, progressive educators and naturalists believed, would encourage school-aged youth and others to better understand and embrace the natural world. "Nature-study cultivates the child's imagination, since there are so many wonderful and true stories that he may read with his own eyes, which affect his imagination as much as does fairy lore, at the same time nature study cultivates in him a perception and a regard for what is true, and the power to express it," wrote Anna Botsford Comstock, a natural science artist and educator whose 1911 book, *Handbook of Nature Study*, was a classroom staple for teachers and others. (The book is still in print.). "Nature study gives the child practical and helpful knowledge. It makes him familiar with nature's ways and forces, so that he is not so helpless in the presence of natural misfortune and disasters."

Mary fully embraced nature study. When she had to give up Camp Fire Girls in Hopedale when she went to Radcliffe, a November 13, 1916, letter from the organization's New York offices thanked her for "the splendid interest you have taken in this work . . . . I can well imagine that you are proud of your girls, and it is a pity that you cannot continue with them." But some of those Hopedale girls wanted to continue their connection to Mary. Sixteen-year-old Frances Darling thought Mary would want "to know what your C. F. girls are doing." The Hopedale Camp Fire chapter, she wrote in a January 28, 1918, letter, had a new leader, Miss Starrett.

> Miss Starrett read the description of how we named the Camp Fire, and chose its symbol, and your description of the girls. I think it was the first time we have had it read since you left us. We had kind of forgotten some parts of it and it seemed nicer than ever.
>
> We have bought some wool and the different girls are knitting things for three soldiers that Miss Starrett knows, now in France . . . . Another awfully good time . . . was when we went into the woods at that big oak tree (where we got the bananas from the fruit man, do you remember?). It was lovely and cold and crisp and we were just glad to be alive . . . . I'm sure the girls would send their love if they knew I was writing to you so I'm going to for them.

No matter where she was working, Mary pushed young people outdoors. "Especially after a long winter, Mrs. Blair would tell us to go outside," Bob Tuttle said as we talked in front of his former school on a bright fall afternoon. He pointed to a tall tree close to the building. "Mrs. Blair said, 'As soon as you learn and can recite these poems, you can go home.' So I climbed up that tree and memorized whatever verses she wanted. And I still remember all of them."

14. Recess at the West Epping schoolhouse, 1943.

At her school, rope swings hung from a big spruce tree and Mary organized outdoor games and activities. In the winter, students took to skis and sleds in front of the school. On hot days, they went home for bathing suits, with Mary leaving a blackboard message, "School in session at the swimming hole." The winter version was skating on the nearby Lamprey River

Mary's outdoor parades sometimes marched far beyond the swimming hole. She led her young students on miles-long hikes that began at her house, meandered through the woods along the Pawtuckaway River to Stingy River Road, and then up another road to the lake. The girls slept inside the bungalow and the boys camped outside. Far from shuddering at the memory of those rustic overnights and long walks—the hike to Arcady was more than five miles each way, much of it uphill—former students found them exhilarating, Ramona Stevens told me.

> We would all start at her house on a Friday afternoon.
> Mrs. Blair would provide baskets with eggs, chicken and
> homemade bread. We'd get to the bungalow and cook over a
> wood fire. She'd make her stew or her corn chowder. She had an
> old boat she'd let us use and taught a lot of us how to swim right
> there. Then we'd walk all the way back on Sunday.

I don't know how long it took us to walk that far because we had such a good time that we didn't even think about the time. The whole way, Mrs. Blair talked about everything. The flowers, the rocks, the undergrowth—she loved it all and it rubbed off on me.

Surely, some of these adolescents must have gone at least a little astray, I suggested. "Mrs. Blair was so well respected none of us would have done anything wrong," said Ramona, who said Mary's example inspired her to become a teacher herself. Mary pasted onto an Arcady wall a quote from Victorian art critic and social thinker John Ruskin that neatly summarized her philosophy. "See that your children be taught not only the labors of the earth, but the loveliness of it." (She could have also posted naturalist Louis Agassiz' succinct admonition, "Study nature, not books.").

When Bob Tuttle returned to New Hampshire after his retirement, he drove that same road that he and his classmates hiked with Mary to Arcady so long ago. "I kept saying to myself, My God—we walked this. We'd be this long parade of kids just straggling along but I have no recollection of anyone complaining."

15. Mary's students on log bridge across the Pawtuckaway River.

Perhaps he was among the students in a photograph from the early 1930s standing atop a "corduroy" bridge made from rows of logs spanning the Pawtuckaway River. The girls wear skirts and the boys also appear dressed for school. Three boys dangle their legs over the water; splashes mark where their rocks hit the river. Maybe this was one of Mary's relatively short outings from the school more than a mile away. Or maybe it was just a pause on one of those much longer treks to Arcady. Currents and time have washed away the old bridge's logs but its stone abutments remain. I envision that gaggle of Mary's students every time I pass them on my own walks.

"A great spiritual uplift."

After permanently returning to New Hampshire, Mary worked with other youth organizations, including 4-H and the American Youth Foundation (AYF), which was formed in 1925, the same year that AYF opened Camp Merrowvista near New Hampshire's Lake Ossipee.

AYF was founded as a "non-profit Christian leadership training organization," emphasizing "the philosophy of four-fold balanced living through mental, social, physical, and spiritual growth." Mary was attracted to AYF's outdoor focus; she may also have been drawn to its mission of helping "American young people to live *wholesome Christian lives*," as a 1933 AYF publication put it. Mary's only journal reference to AYF came when she tried to fill in some long gaps in her narrative, including the names of the Merrowvista cabins in which she stayed.

> December 27, 1935
>
> Well, might as well be right about making a few records. I always wish that I had made more of them for I forget very easily the years in which things happened. For instance, when did I first go to Merrowvista. I think that it must have been seven years ago. Let me see. Penobscot—Seneca, Algonquin, Mohawk—twice in Kimmie Kabin and once in No. 10. Yes I have been there seven years . . . . I hope to go back for my 8th summer—if they want me and I can go. There is a great spiritual uplift there.

She did go back. According to AYF records, Mary was on the all-volunteer "faculty" at camps for both older girls and younger girls through 1940. She was "Camp Mother" for many of those years and oversaw numerous activities and classes, including 4-H leadership, woodcraft, dramatics, nature, the geology of New Hampshire, outdoor activities, and swimming. She was also "involved in the Questionnaire process, which interviewed campers and wrote prescriptions for improving activities in the four-fold balance of life, a counseling role" and was a "cabin leader," according to an email from AYF archivist Jan Strube. Mary's grand niece Nancy Perry—her sister Mabel's granddaughter—attended the camp in 1937. Merrowvista is one of two summer camps still operated by AYF, which is "now an interfaith organization welcoming people from all backgrounds and traditions," according to its website.

Mary also became one of New Hampshire's longest serving 4-H leaders. She formed the "We Sew Some" club for girls in Epping in 1918 and in 1925 launched the Greenwood Forestry Club for boys. Even as she neared her 90th birthday, Mary continued meeting with her girls' club, according to an October 9, 1968, *Manchester Union-Leader* article about her "never-ending and rewarding association" with 4-H.

> Mrs. Blair explains that she was drawn into 4-H club work because she felt the need, as a teacher, of far more contacts with the children of her community. Her early work in 4-H was primarily instructional aid in cooking and sewing for girls and eventually agricultural projects for the boys.
>
> Then she fostered a wider program of 4-H activities, and they were many by 1925, like nature study and development of music and drama. . . . Mrs. Blair takes deserved pride in the fact that she was a pioneer in the 4-H camping movement, that today has . . . more than 2,000 youngsters in the state, coming from all ten counties, get deep woods vacations . . . .
>
> With a wealth of knowledge to impart to her club youngsters . . . and with a philosophy that rates 4-H as "freedom of choice for a child," this enthusiastic rural lady has compiled a record of accomplishments in her chosen field about a yard wide and a mile long!

National 4-H honored that record in 1959 when Mary flew to Chicago as one of three recipients of the national "Friend of 4-H Award." At the age of seventy-eight, Mary, who never even drove a car, was less than thrilled about getting on an airplane, recalled Elizabeth Bourne, who joined her on that trip. "She found a scrap of paper and gave a note to someone in case she never made it back," Beth said. "We traveled back from Chicago by train. I took her to Niagara Falls on our way back."

About twenty years younger than Mary, Beth Bourne was also a long-time 4-H leader. When I interviewed her in the mid-1990s at her family home in Bourne, Mass., she was retired but still active with 4-H. Beth taught on Cape Cod but moved to New Hampshire to become the Rockingham County Extension Service's 4-H Club agent in 1926, a post she held until she retired in 1969. She quickly bonded with Mary, with whom she set up 4-H clubs, camps, and chapters. The two also worked together at Camp Merrowvista.

16. Mary, left, with other Camp Merrowvista "faculty."

Together, the two women helped create the first outdoor 4-H camp in New Hampshire at Hedding Campground in Epping in 1930. Six leaders, including Beth and Mary, supervised thirty-four girls that first year. "Each leader was cook for one day," according to Beth's hand-written report. "Five girls worked their way." Mary instructed handicrafts at the "Girls Camp." Beth kept meticulous records, including about expenses, which in 1932 totaled $9.79 (about $170 in today's dollars), including, "Bottle of shellac .25; 6 cans paint .60, 2 doz pencils .24; nuts for fudge .15; Bird books for girls .50 5 yds white cloth 20; 30 coat hangers 1.15."

The 1932 4-H camp, which lasted one week and attracted 24 girls and 14 boys, featured "a new course in Camp Craft" taught by Mary. "It included outdoors goodmanners, camping along the road, traveling by auto, hiking, building fires, what to do if lost etc., and proved very interesting," according to Beth's notes. The 4-H summer camp moved to bigger and better facilities in 1937 at Bear Hill Pond Camp, which was built by the New Deal's Civilian Conservation Corps. Attendance at that Allentown, N.H., camp grew to forty-nine girls and forty-two boys. Mary, who taught nature, was among the session's twenty leaders. The camp had one problem that summer, noted the camp's annual report. "Evening programs and recreation were not as interesting as usual due to our being afraid to have treasure or scavenger hunts because of Rattlesnakes."

"Mary was so advanced both as a teacher and as a 4-H leader," Beth told me. "She even taught me. Everything I know about ferns I learned with her at Merrowvista."

Much later in life, Mary paid the tuition for local young people to attend Merrowvista. Her friend and colleague Beth Bourne also created a scholarship fund for college-bound youth with 4-H backgrounds. Beth is buried on Cape Cod. The 4-H logo adorns her simple gravestone.

Chapter 12

Arcady: "The peace of the pines"

"Of all my possessions," Mary wrote in an undated note, "my little camp is the dearest to my heart."

The origins of Arcady, her Pawtuckaway Lake bungalow, are unclear. Some people told me that it was a family gift to Mary after her graduation from Sanborn Seminary, though that is unlikely since Mary graduated in 1900 and the bungalow was not built until 1906. Another more probable version is that Mary's parents built the cabin as a fresh air retreat for Mary's brother Albert, who suffered from tuberculosis.

In any case, Arcady was the first cottage built on the lake's Gove's Cove, which is reached via a long dirt road that remains much as it was when wagons bumped their way over it. Mary boasted that Arcady was built with $80 of lumber (a little more than $2,300 in current dollars). Some of the wood was processed at the Folsom mill and transported by sled across the frozen lake to the building site. Mary was proud that she cobbled together much of the inside contents from a myriad of original places and purposes.

In an early photograph, the exterior board and batten pine boards look fresh. The porch is unfinished, a door resting sideways on the floor awaiting installation. Three women sit on the porch steps; the one on the right is Mary, with a dog on her lap.

Almost everything around Arcady has changed since then. The few remaining small camps from Mary's era are dwarfed by newer and much bigger houses, with armadas of float boats and other water craft tied to their docks. But Arcady itself is much as it was in its earliest days, except for the slanting low kitchen added to the back in the 1940s. The saltbox-style bungalow is just feet from water's edge amid the grove's tall white pines, the needles of which cushion the ground and seep onto the porch floor. Mary sat under those pines as she wrote in her journal. The two small bedrooms off the living area are little changed from when their first occupants swatted away mosquitoes and slept to the nighttime chorus of summer. The inside walls are darkened by age and the high ceiling rises over the main living area and its smoke-smudged fireplace. A four-inch piece of stone that Mary found by the Folsom mill dam and that she believed to be a hand-notched hammer-head is still on the mantel.

17-18. Arcady—paddles ready by the steps—as it looked around 1913 and (bottom) in 2021.

Mary's first journal reference of the camp came on August 6, 1908. The rock she mentioned remains an underwater hazard.

> The Bungalow itself is all that I ever dreamed of and more. But it hasn't been quite the land of the lotus eaters that I had

planned for—not quite the dreamy peaceful idle days of rest
and reading. But perhaps I have enjoyed the unexpected better.
It began the first Sunday by my getting hung up on a rock,
forgetting how to swim and nearly drowning. Ugh—that cool
green water so far over my head, down, down, down wondering if
I could hold my breath until the rising impulse came, and the one
more breath of blessed air, one glimpse of light and down into
the darkness. At last the welcome grasp of Marian's arm, then
the dim outline of the canoe and Eben's voice. Honest when I
washed my face next day I had the nausea.

Mary soon christened the bungalow with a name that linked her
interests in the mythological and natural worlds. She was fascinated by
Pan, the Greek god of the wild, whose homeland was a pastoral paradise
in the Greek Peloponnese region of Arcadia, the probably inspiration
for the name "Arcady." People from all strands of Mary's life joined her
there. Former students visited; some even honeymooned there, including
Bob Tuttle and his wife Dot. "We were in college at the time and the war
was on," he remembered as he and his wife returned to Arcady with me
one day in the early 2000s. They gazed at writing they added to a wall
to mark their honeymoon stay: "Oct. 7-10, 1942. Trip Subsequent to
Marriage. Bob-Dot Tuttle".

The Tuttles returned several times after their honeymoon, once with
a new family member. "If possible, the lobsters have improved. This
time, a new initiate to the peace, joy, and happiness that is Arcady," read
the inscription marking that August 24, 1962, visit. Members of the
West Epping Women's Club and others with whom Mary worked or
socialized also came, often enjoying the lobster feasts that overflowed
from plates piled atop the small dining table.

Folsom and other family members were regular guests. Mary and
Edmond, and the bungalow, outdid themselves on August 29, 1929,
when they hosted the Eighteenth Annual Reunion of the Folsom
Family Association, for which Mary served that year as Recording
Secretary. Blissfully unaware of the market crash that would shake the
world just two months later, Mary's official report of the lakeside event

19. Mary and a visiting Arcadian in the bungalow's tiny kitchen.

noted that from across the country, "Seventy of the family and several of their guests found their way to the rocky shores of Pawtuckaway, there to greet each other beneath the tall pines and to establish or renew ties of kinship and of friendliness."

The day's agenda included a presentation by Mary about "the origin of the word 'Pawtuckaway' according to the old Indian legends." Another Folsom offered "an interesting account of the Indian massacre in Nottingham, in which three men, one of them Nathaniel Folsom, lost their lives a short mile from the place where the paper was read." I tried to imagine how little Arcady and Mary could host such a large gathering, though according to her report, "The good neighbors of the grove added greatly to the pleasure of the occasion by the offer of boats and chairs and extra cups of coffee."

Even with fewer folks in attendance, the bungalow buzzed with activity. From Arcady, Mary and her merry bands ventured out on land and water. Mary described one such outing to the nearby Pawtuckaway Mountains (so-called, though they stand at only about 1,000 feet).

August 24, 1908

We went in the canoe to the head of Mountain Brook Cove
and hiding our canoe in the thicket followed a path out to the
road and walked about two miles until we came to the valley
between the upper and lower mountains.

From there it is an easy climb to the summit of the lower
mountain from which a good view is obtained. Returning about
five, Grace and I completed the day by a dip in the lake and a
more or less quiet night's sleep. That was the night that the
crowd stayed up all night and had the fish fry over to Lake View
to which we weren't invited. We didn't really care a continental
but pretended to feel terribly injured and it was funny to see how
apologetic the men were next day.

There were various other days and nights to be remembered.
One when the men came over all dressed up and we clothed
ourselves likewise to receive them—our ordinary costume being
bathing suits. Then we played whist and had Welsh Rarebit and
were the most properest crowd I ever seen.

After "awakening somewhere round three o'clock in the morning"
from a nap in her canoe, Mary pondered what she had heard about some
of her male guests.

I had a revelation of a man's character in the story of another
girl, told with an unconsciousness either real or assumed. If real, it
betokens a modesty that I didn't think men possessed, if assumed,
one may at least commend the chivalry that prompted such
seeming consciousness. It is largely possible that the moonlight
and the water had something to do with my crediting so much to
the telling of the story, or rather its teller.

Even in the off-season, Arcady occupied "a fair sample of the stuff in
my gray cells," she wrote Anne on April 5, 1910. "I drove up with father
the other day and everything looked so pretty with the even covering
of fresh pine needles over all. The ice was all out except a long greenish
white strip from the point to the islands. On either side the water looked

blue and sparkling and very tempting to a certain green canoe that was longing for a bath. But the canoe managed to resist the temptation."

When she turned thirty-one, Mary used her annual birthday entry to describe a typical Arcady season.

> July 8th Again 1912
> Again. Oh yes. The years come round more quickly than they did in the glad days of old when I was seventeen and every year had twelve good months and true in it. Time goes so swiftly now that it seems but a little while since I closed camp and left these Arcadian shades with the prospect of a year's work before me. Gee—why can't it be a year's play.
> We've been in camp since the 17th of June. On the whole it has been very near the ideal that I used to dream of. Very, very quiet, long days of rest and idleness, a day ended by a canoe ride or an hour by the blazing fire. It's been a terribly lazy land. It's surprising how easy and natural it is to do absolutely nothing but eat and sleep—and wash dishes and cook meals . . . . There was a howling crowd of Raymondites in Gove's . . . . They all got indecently and disrespectably drunk. But we minded them as little as possible.

Mary linked her loves of Anne and Arcady.

> The most vivid memory in my mind is the night . . . . four of us camped round the fire on cushions, flinging cones into the fireplace. First thing we knew we were all asleep. Then we awoke and the boys and Anne sang. It is strange but many of my most vivid memories are of moments half between waking and sleeping or sleeping and waking. Monday we marathoned to the mountains in 4 3/4 hours. Some going! The boys had just fifteen minutes to eat, dress and pack when they returned. Then they drove off cheerfully waving sandwiches at us. Anne and I settled down on the couch hammock, said "Oh what a good time we've had" and waked up some after sunset. I felt sniffy when the boys departed.

Arcady's rhythms of blissful days, lobster feasts, canoe trips by sun or moon, and visits by "ye olde garde" and others continued for decades. But age was catching up to Mary. On July 8, 1961, she inscribed a brief birthday entry onto an Arcady door rather than into her journal. "I am an octogenarian," she scrawled, adding, "Too cold to swim!"

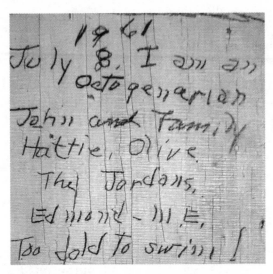

20. An Arcady door records a birthday milestone, visitors—and the weather.

By the late 1960s, Mary began to ponder the future of her sacred space. Decades after Mildred Brown and Mary were schoolmates, Mary had recruited Mildred's daughter Pearl to teach in "the other room" of her West Epping school. Mary praised Pearl in her journal.

> She is a great happiness in the lives of all of us. She is very social-minded and realizes the needs of the unfortunate here in West Epping as much as I do. The children "adore her. I would have thought once that I should have felt a little—well—call it jealousy to see them clinging about another teacher as they have to me—but there isn't a bit of it. I'm just happy to think that such a friend has been raised up for them.

As the relationship between Mary and Pearl "evolved to one of peers," Mary decided to entrust Arcady to Pearl, said Pearl's daughter Janice, who lived with her parents and grandmother in Hampton, N.H. Once, Mary unexpectedly invited Janice to spend the night at Arcady.

> I said yes, probably surprising everyone, including my shy young self, and I found myself alone with two people I didn't know very well. I was a little afraid of Edmond, who was very different from any adult male in my life, a little gruff and more interested in a radio broadcast of Red Sox baseball than my presence. Mary felt like a kindred spirit, despite the difference in our ages. I felt seen, accepted, and understood by her and I loved her dearly for that.

One particular detail from that visit stands out, Janice continued.

> Someone stopped by to visit and cigars and a bottle of hard liquor appeared (I had never been around either—Baptists don't indulge). I can clearly picture May sitting in her Morris chair in a slightly reclined position, shot glass in one hand and cigar in the other, looking relaxed and happy and regaling her guests with her delightful sense of humor.

By the mid-1960s, Mary was finding it difficult to maintain the bungalow and to keep paying its tax bill. She made the difficult decision to sell. But to whom? Many people in the Epping area wanted first refusal, which overwhelmed Mary, said Janice.

> Perhaps it was in talking it over with my mother that a solution took form. In any event, my mother, promising to love and cherish it, took out a loan and bought Arcady. My mother was true to her word, as she too loved the peace of the pines and the connection to her dear friend. Under her care, only minor changes and updates were made when absolutely needed.

Janice and her mother, who taught in nearby Newfields, N.H., spent occasional nights at Arcady, though her father could not ("A dairy farm demands hard work over long hours so he rarely had time away," Janice explained.). In 1983, her mother, "finding herself also at an age where she could no longer manage it or afford the taxes, offered Arcady to my husband Bill and me and we have been its stewards ever since."

Many of the people who were important to Mary had warm memories of Arcady. Two of my most essential guides, her nephew, Mr. Perry, and Edmond's niece, Jean Pye, regretted that decades had passed since their last visits. I wanted to fix that. So on a crisp fall day in 1993, Bill and Janice Jassmond and I waited for the two of them and their spouses to return to Arcady.

Mr. Perry arrived first with his wife Anne and her daughter Nancy, followed a half hour later by the Pyes. Sitting at water's edge, Mr. Perry pointed to that same hazardous rock about which Mary wrote. "Aunt May nearly drowned there," he said. "She sunk two or three times, and about the third time, someone saw her and saved her life."

Inside, he studied the writings on the walls and doors. He beamed when he spotted barely legible script from 1911 that named "The small Perrys," one of whom was his six-year-old self. Mr. Perry found his name on other doors and walls. "That's my writing," he said of some 1957 scribbling, which also listed a visitor named Diane. "Were you here with another girl?" his wife asked. "I'm not telling you," Mr. Perry replied. He recalled an early visit with his brother. "We went out in the lake a little bit. The two of us moved around in the boat—and the first thing we knew, Aunt May appeared. 'Don't you ever move around in a boat because it could tip over and you'd drown!' she yelled to us. We never moved again in a boat after that. I also remember her lying on this couch early in the morning. She was telling stories, using the shadow of her hands to make animals on the door."

Jean Pye, in whose Connecticut home Mary spent the next to last year of her life, also "had so many good times here," she said. "Aunt May would be in her canoe and affect these Indian head bands. And she was determined that I learn from her about all the wild flowers and ferns.

21. Mary's nephew, Richard Hunt Perry, points to where Mary marked his visit eight decades earlier.

I also remember her cooking for crowds, often lobsters. They made chicken for me because I didn't like lobster at the time."

Jean recalled Mary's regret when age limited her ability to get to the bungalow and even into the woods in Epping.

> On one of my last visits to the old house in Epping, Mary was walking out along the trail along a brook where the cardinal flowers used to grow. She used a cane, was quite feeble. We took a chair along and she sat down part way and said it was so good to be back up here. She said she had so many memories of Pawtuckaway to sustain her. I can just see her with a canoe going out there, when she was probably close to 70, if not older. And swimming and camping on the island all by herself. She'd sleep all night with a blanket in the canoe.

Mary would have welcomed the return of long-ago Arcadians, including descendants of Anne Reed. "You'll need no picture to bring back to you the memory worked here," Mary wrote in her Idylls of Arcady "letter" to Anne. "The memory of good comrades—loyal companions clean-limbed, clean-hearted lads who have possessed that key to Arcady that I've spoken of, an understanding heart."

After the Jassmonds moved to Oregon in 2019, I occasionally drove over to repair screens, clear pine needles and branches from the roof, and to otherwise check on things. It felt good and right to help keep up the old place. And the pay and benefits were unbeatable.

Alone, I absorbed the stillness of the off-season. Even on busy summer days, I could imagine away the drone of motor boats and relive the magic of decades past, with Mary very much present. Many of the items in the nooks and on the shelves were hers, from kitchen pots and chairs to a Camp Merrowvista plaque. A 1962 National Education Association pamphlet, *Teaching About Communism: Guidelines for Junior and Senior High School Teachers*, remained on a table for my curious reading. From the porch I looked to my right past the hanging hammock, to the stand of pines where someone—Anne? Edmond?—took that wonderful photograph of Mary writing in one of her journals. Her shadow was still there.

No matter how many times I turned the skeleton key to enter Arcady, I was transported to a more serene past. Sometimes I spotted wall writing that I had somehow missed or forgotten. Much of it had become unreadable, leaving pieces of my Mary saga forever blank. Other names that popped off the walls and doors became my own Arcady regulars. These members of "ye olde garde" —Tuttles, Perrys, Reeds, Folsoms, Pyes—became my own regular companions at Arcady, just as they had been Mary's.

"I think I'd find it easy to haunt Arcady," Mary wrote on July 8, 1912. Sitting in the armchair from which she held court with Indian lore and other tales, I could almost see her moving about. I could hear the scratch of her pen filling a wall with her long ode to Pan. I listened for the nighttime yips and whispers of giggling grade schoolers and the Gentle Knights in their tents by lake.

In "To Arcady," Mary described her "joyous visions of bygone days."

> Oh where did you come from, Arcady fair
> With a wild rose caught in your dusky hair
>   And your garments softly flowing?
> I came from a haunt in Arcady
> Where many a rose is blooming
> Oh where is the road to Arcady
> Since so many there are growing.
>
> Oh follow the note of the hermit thrush
> Whose dear tones thrill thru the twilight hush
>   From the dim old forest ringing
> He trills from the gates of Arcady
> To guide us by his singing
>   To dwell again in those Arcadian shades
>   To fling aside all rule and form and care
>   To wander freely thru the forest glades
>   As flies the bird untrammeled thru the air

"Arcady has always felt close to being a sacred space, one whose energy we also did not want to disturb or modify," said Janice. "Mary's relationship to the bungalow was deep and existed on many levels. Both energetically and concretely, here is recorded so much of Mary's life. The hand-carved plaque over the fireplace—'Behold, good friend, beneath these pines, a hearth that loves a guest. Where he who walks may wait at ease, and he who runs may rest'—always touches my heart and seems to speak to the need for that ineffable state to endure."

Chapter 13

"Love will dream and faith will hold."

Pat and Miriam Jackson had an unexpected visitor shortly after they moved to West Epping in the mid-1960s. Knocking on their door, Mary Folsom Blair said she had come by to greet the new occupants of the house that had been in her family since it was built in 1793. She went on to give a brief local history lesson.

"This was interesting, but we still didn't understand why she had come," Pat recalled when he and I met in 1992 at the now-long-gone Loaf & Ladle restaurant across from the office of his public relations firm in Exeter, N.H. Mary's real reason soon emerged—she hoped that these newcomers might become members of the West Epping Meeting of the Religious Society of Friends, better known as the Quakers.

Mary needed such recruits. By the time of her visit to the Jacksons, Mary, then in her eighties, was the last active Quaker in Epping, and that was simply unacceptable to this direct descendant of Joshua Folsom, her great grandfather and Epping's first Quaker. The West Epping Meeting House was built in 1851 on land donated by another Folsom ancestor. But by the 1960s, most of West Epping's Quakers had moved away or died off. The simple white building on Friend Street had not hosted regular meetings for decades. "By 1970, Mary was so determined to keep her world in order that she sits in the Meeting House one day a year and is proselytizing others to keep the meeting alive," said Pat. Mary sometimes wore the cap and shawl that belonged to her grandmother.

Mary's determination to sustain the West Epping Meeting was not just driven by religious zeal, according to Pat. Rather, under Quaker procedures, were the West Epping Meeting to close, the Meeting and its assets would "lay down" to the nearest Friends Quarterly Meeting, which in this case would be the one in Seabrook, N.H. That prospect chilled Mary for reasons far more personal than theological. The Seabrook meeting, Pat explained, was associated with Quaker poet John Greenleaf Whittier, against whom the Folsoms, including Mary, held a generational grudge.

22. Mary wears her Quaker grandmother's cap and shawl.

Whittier often traveled to Red Oak Hill in Epping to visit Rowena Thyng, a local school teacher 16 years his junior. "It has long been thought that Whittier and Rowena were more than friends," wrote Epping historian Madelyn Williamson. "Their initials, set within joined hearts, were discovered carved on an oak tree behind the . . . barn. Seventy years later, in 1941, the same initials and heart design were found inside the house in Rowena's old room."

By 1840, Whittier, whose first poem was published by abolitionist William Lloyd Garrison in 1826, was a leader in the anti-slavery movement, even getting stoned by an anti-abolitionist mob in Concord, N.H., in 1835. Epping Quakers likely shared Whittier's abolitionist ardor, but they came to resent his political dogmatism, according to Pat, who said his account came directly from his conversations with Mary. "Whenever Whittier came to Epping, he lectured everyone, including Mary's grandfather, that no good Quaker could be a Democrat because Democrats were associated with the South and slavery and the Confederacy." But the Folsoms were stalwart Democrats and two Folsom generations later, Mary was not about to let her West Epping meeting lay down to one connected to Whittier.

Others to whom I spoke were less certain about this supposed Folsom animosity toward Whittier. But whatever her motivation, Mary succeeded in getting the Jacksons and others to become regular attendees of the West Epping Friends Meeting. Pat's second marriage was held in the Meeting House in 1974. So too was his memorial service in 2001, at which I read an excerpt from Mary's journals. And he and some of his family are buried in the Friends cemetery along with Mary and other Epping Quakers.

For all her commitment to the West Epping Meeting, Mary's early journals contain little reference to her Quakerism. She did attend Meeting while growing up, as attested by a 1904 letter from a woman named Alice Winslow. Written in the "thee and thou" style used by more conservative Quakers, Winslow's letter was religious in tone and content. She wondered whether Mary, then a twenty-three-year-old teacher in Epping, might be receptive to religious messages. "Some weeks have slipped away since I took thy card—& often my eye has rested upon it—and so reminded me of my desire to know thee better—for as I looked unto thy face during the meeting my heart went out toward thee."

23. Screen shot of *Chronicle* interview with Pat Jackson in the West Epping Meeting House, 2000. —Courtesy of WCVB-TV

Unlike Winslow and other more traditional Quakers, including her father, Mary used "plain language" in her writing and conversation. She also often attended non-Quaker Protestant services. Her 1918 marriage was in front of a Catholic priest in a Catholic church. And when Mary died in 1973, Epping acquaintances who had assisted her in her last months arranged for her funeral to be held in a fundamentalist church, not in the Meeting House, though Mary is buried with her Quaker ancestors and next to her husband Edmond in the Friends Cemetery.

Quakeress Mary was also an active member of the Epping chapter of the Daughters of the American Revolution, not exactly an organization known for its pacifist views. Mary sought to square being both a good Quaker and a patriotic DAR member in one of the historic pageants she wrote in 1931 about the Town of Epping. Her handwritten script reflected Mary's core belief that a society's best defense is education, not arms. The play included a Revolutionary War scene set in the home of Mary's great great grandfather, Joshua Folsom (played, Mary noted in the margin, "by a direct descendant," her nephew John Folsom).

163

The narrator set the scene.

> Not everyone in Epping felt the thrill and fervor of the call to
> arms. In the western part of the town early in the century had
> lived a few members of that society known among themselves as
> "Friends," but better known to the world's people as "Quakers."
> Friend Joshua Folsom and Abigail, his wife, are interrupted at
> their evening devotions.

A neighbor had come to warn the Folsoms that they were suspected
of being pro-British Tories. "There is a mob coming to do you damage,"
the neighbor said. "I've brought you a gun to defend yourself."
Moments later, another knock is heard. It is Revolutionary War General
Joseph Cilley. Born in nearby Nottingham, N.H., Cilley was a customer
of Folsom's grist mill.

> Gen. Cilley: You are an honest man, too honest to be a Tory.
> It cannot be possible that you are a Tory, although I've been
> so informed.
> Joshua: Thee has been misinformed. I am not a Tory. But the
> members of the Society of Friends do not believe that arms are
> the best means of settling a quarrel.
> Gen. Cilley: But would you not take up arms to defend your
> country?
> Joshua: The best defense of any country is education and
> understanding and right living. It is only during peaceful times
> that progress is made. I fain would hear the bugles of battle blow
> the marches of universal peace and good will.
> Gen. Cilley: Impossible! It is a wild dream. Do you think the
> King is right in this matter?
> Joshua: It is borne unto me very strongly that the colonists are
> right, and the right shall prevail.
> Gen. Cilley: They were coming tonight to rob you, to burn
> your mill, and to destroy your property; but I shall make haste to
> head them off. They'll not harm you except over my dead body.

Mary was molded by her Quaker foundation. The Friends' early respect for female equality helped shape her determination to become an independent thinker and feminist (a label from which she might have recoiled). Two of Mary's great aunts were Quaker ministers. In her classroom and the wider community, Mary practiced the Quaker commitment to improve conditions for those in need. Former student Bob Tuttle, who grew up next door to the Meeting House, occasionally attended meetings there. "Whether you were a Friend or not, that was the church in West Epping. That's where you went," he said. "When regular ministers couldn't make it from nearby towns, Mrs. Blair would conduct the services."

Mary left behind a valuable chronicle of Quakerism and her family in the form of a lengthy presentation "Given for the Alliance" on January 18, 1911. It is unclear to what "Alliance" Mary gave her talk, but she felt it worthy enough to transcribe it by hand, filling thirty pages of her journal. The presentation, which appears in full in Appendix 2, offers a window into Mary's childhood and the Quaker ways she observed growing up.

> The Quaker of ye olden time has left us, and his descendants have so fallen into the ways of the world's people that there is no perceptible difference between them. When we see good things that they advocated we would wonder why Quakerism hasn't become more dominant. They were pioneers in so many great movements.... Today the cry of the suffragette is loud in the land. They are appealing for rights held by the fair Quakeress for the last two centuries and a half for the society has ever recognized that where woman is not the superior she _is_ the equal of man.

Mary's description of the West Epping Meeting House could be written today.

> [T]he little white meeting house on the plains still stands, plain and solid and substantial, fitting type of the men and women who worshipped within its walls. Its interior is very plain. There are no rare and costly windows thru which the mellow light may

165

fall, no graceful arch, no solemn organ tones, only the clean white walls, the glympse of God's own sky thru the high windows and the solemn stillness save for the murmur of the wind in the great pines outside, or the lilting song of a bird . . . . In that simple meeting place was an atmosphere of reverence that is not always present in costly temples.

24. "[T]he glympse of God's own sky thru the high windows" of the Meeting House.

Mary detailed the design of a Quaker Meeting House, including "the high-facing seat where the elders and ministers sit . . . [and] a partition about three feet high running thru the middle and dividing the men's side from the women's. A sliding shutter can be rolled down to meet this partition thus completely separating the two parts. This is used when there is a business meeting and the men and women wish to consider matters separately."

Continuing her presentation, Mary recalled her Quaker relatives, including her "grandfather and my grandmother, this great aunt and another great great aunt, all well over their eighties, sitting on the high facing seats in solemn and dignified array and very imposing they seemed to me. The 'young folks' of sixty and upwards were on the lower facing seats."

Visitors were sometimes befuddled by Quaker silence.

> More often than not . . . the meeting was a silent one, for unless there happened to be a visiting friend present the Spirit seldom moved. However I remember well one First Day a number of the World's people visited the quiet little meeting place and to their unaccustomed ideas the silence seemed strange and the plain costumes funny and the seats very uncomfortable. So their behavior became somewhat unseemly and the spirit moved my grandfather to arise and deliver a somewhat stirring homily on the evils of curiosity, taking for his text 'What went ye out for to see.' The soothing effect on the world's people was quite marked.

To prepare for monthly meeting, Mary's grandmother spent days cleaning and cooking "enough to feed a regiment," the presentation continued. "There used to be fifteen or twenty in the old days return for dinner, sweet faced old ladies in their best silk gowns and finest lace caps, somewhat stern faced men in straight-colared coats and broad brimmed hats."

Mary next described her grandfather's garden, which included "clumps of gorgeous tiger lilies" that I still pass every summer behind where the Folsom barn stood. For Quakers, Mary wrote, flowers were "their one way of expressing their love for color and beauty." She recalled a bridge of "gray, moss grown planks" that was "a somewhat uncertain pathway" to plants growing "wherever the sun or soil suited them."

> In the early spring time long rows of scarlet tulips lifted their cups to the sun, the snow-drops bloomed under the window, the purple and white lilacs loaded the heavy air with fragrance. The dear white daffys, my mother's favorite, pushed its green shoots up thru the moist earth. [In the summer] peonies bloomed and beds of pansies and portaluccas, zinnias and moss pinks and petunias held sway. There was no time in the year when some fascinating green thing couldn't be found within these garden walls."

167

Relatives from near and far visited Mary's home when they attended Quaker meetings. "The subdued click of needles kept up a pleasant accompaniment to the exchange of wit and wisdom, quaint legends and thrilling adventures," including those of a famous uncle, David E. Folsom. Raised in Epping, health reasons made him move west, where he helped to map what would become Yellowstone National Park.

Mary was relieved that she had duly transcribed her Quaker memories into her journal. "There, the Lord be thanked, I have at last finished copying that thing," she wrote on April 22, 1911. "I'm glad to have the things father told about secure, also a partial description of Grandsire's garden. What a wonderful old higledy-piggledy place it was, and I'll wager I'm the only one left in the family to realize it."

Mary did manage to keep the West Epping Meeting active. Shortly after her death in 1973, regular meetings resumed. The little white meeting house still stands. Mary's long-ago knock on the Jacksons' door was answered.

Chapter 14

"We enjoy each other's society."

Mary's journaling dwindled after she settled into marriage and teaching upon her return to West Epping in 1918. Mary was still writing, however, scripting and producing historic plays and pageants. She was also busy with her outdoor youth activities, the Quaker Meeting, and, most of all, her blissful summers at Arcady. Mary did occasionally return to her story-telling ways in her journal.

> March 30, 1927
> Mr. Meader has been looking for a wife. He has a pile of matrimonial journals a foot high to help him. She came to-day. The village learned about it and as many as possible were on hand. Mr. M dressed himself in new overalls to meet her. She came with a trunk, suit case, umbrella and hat box, looked Mr. M over, refused to consider either his camp or a tenement, and departed on the next train. Poor Mr. Meader.

She also continued to record special moments, such as "the thrill" of attending her first country fair in 1927. "The smells and the crowds and the cattle, the fakirs all full swing, the dare devil stunts. I enjoyed it." But Mary was feeling her age. The ice upon which she once so breezily skated betrayed her, leading to a broken wrist in 1929, when she was forty-eight. "I suppose I shouldn't have taken my 170 lbs. skating, especially when I hadn't skate straps," Mary confessed to her journal. "I hope I never break another bone."

The Great Depression and more family deaths compounded her own depression, triggering a bout of self-analysis.

> Jan. 3 1930
> I have been reading the records of past years. What a raving lunatic I was in many ways. I must have been suffering from a Freudian complex a large part of the time. Well, it is not half bad to have it recorded because I can't claim it never was and it helps to understand the present generation by well remembering my own deeds. But there is so much one can be

happy about in the contented years that bring the philosophic mind. It is much happier to sit by the fire playing chess with Edmond than to be moaning under the stars because nobody loved me.

My dear brother, George, died in October—was buried the 24th. Edwin and I are the only ones left of my family. I miss George. I can never recall an unkind or critical word from him. 1929 has in some ways been a hard one for us. Little work. Edwin with few resources, an unpleasant auto mix up. George, Edmond and I, yes, the other house, have been in pretty good health. Much to be thankful for.

Born in 1869, George Franklin Folsom was the oldest of Mary's three surviving siblings after older sister Mabel's death in 1904. He was a store-keeper in West Epping as well as its postmaster. Mary's brother, Edwin Sawyer Folsom, was born a year after George and owned and operated the Folsom mill on the Lamprey River founded by his grandfather. For years, Edwin and his family lived in the house next to the Blairs. Mary's youngest brother, Charles Albert Folsom, was born in 1874 and, like Mary and Mabel, attended Sanborn Seminary. Unlike them, Albert did go on to college, graduating from Dartmouth College, where he was a varsity baseball player, in 1899 and Dartmouth Medical School three years later. He went on to practice medicine in Manchester, N.H., for fifteen years before returning to West Epping, where he died of tuberculosis in 1919.

Mary left her journal blank for nearly six years, when she wrote that her nephew John had found a good job "on a forestry project under the Northeastern Forestry Experiment Station" in New York State. About two years later, John returned to Epping to work with his father at the Folsom family mill. That operation was financially struggling. So too were Edmond and Mary, who was now weary of life.

December 27, 1935
Edmond has been working 2 yrs in April straight time insurance. He began to dislike shop work so much and felt that he could make a good income at insurance. Well, it hasn't

materialized yet, but maybe it will sometime. He has such fine courage that no matter what doesn't happen he is always looking forward to what will. I wish I were built that way.

Sometimes I am so blue and discouraged that I would welcome the end of all things for myself. If I die soon enough it would release enough money to pay the grocer's bill. I can't sleep nights. I've taken to sitting up very late so that I won't wake up and face all the cares that ride me like little devils. It honestly seems as though every resource that I've ever had has just evaporated and nothing to show for it. When we were just married Edmond earned such wonderful pay. Thank God we did put money into modern conveniences which we still have after fifteen years of use. When they wear out we shall not be able to replace them.

Mary calculated her earnings in the margin of the journal. "That makes $1800 a year that we have spent and nothing saved," she lamented ($1,800 in 1935 equals about $34,000 today.). She listed what they had paid for cars over the same period, including a Dodge for a thousand dollars, a Buick for $900, and an Overland for $500. Now they owned a Nash. "It is a most comfortable car but Lord only knows where we will ever find money to buy any more," she wrote. "I guess I'm terribly pessimistic over money matters. I just can't get my budget balanced. If I could only get a few hundred dollars together, pay up the grocery bill and that coal bill and any other bill that I don't know much about . . . . and start even I could keep things going on just my salary.

For decades, an old car from that period has been rusting away deep in the woods just off the path along the river. I've often wondered if it is one of the Blairs' troubled vehicles.

The final entry in the journals of Mary Evelyn Folsom Blair—any other writings likely landed in a dump when her house was cleaned out—came on January 30, 1936. For all the highs and lows since her first words in 1897, Mary was mostly at peace. With the Depression's aftershocks still reverberating, she was happy to have a job. She was even comfortable sharing her school and young people with the teacher in the next room. That teacher was Pearl Marston, to whom Mary would eventually entrust Arcady.

January 30, 1936

"And all night long the snow roared on." This morning the drifts are high, our own paths not shoveled out. The plow has been through many times on the main road. Exeter to Hampton Falls is not yet cleared so Pearl hasn't come. No school to-day. When I say so much about worries and unpleasant things I ought to stop and think of our blessings. Edmond and I have excellent health on the whole. We can eat anything we please in season and feel no inconvenience therefrom . . . .

We enjoy each other's society, like the comforts of our own fireside, enjoy our games of chess and recently of checkers. He is very kind.

I am mighty lucky to retain a school and have that interest and income to fill my days and help grease the wheels. I enjoy the friendship of the boys and girls that have been to school to me.

25. Edmond and Mary play chess in their West Epping home.

Mary Folsom Blair ended her half century teaching career where it began, retiring from the West Epping Rural School in 1951 when she was sixty-nine. More than two hundred people attended a reception in her honor at Epping Town Hall. They represented a cross-section of the town and her life: former students, including several generations of the same family; representatives of 4-H; members of the Daughters of the American Revolution and the West Epping Women's Club, of which Mary was a charter member. The program, emceed by her nephew John Folsom—who had become an educator himself—featured Mary's favorite songs, performed by her final graduating class.

In retirement, Mary remained involved with the Quaker meeting, 4-H, the Daughters of the American Revolution, the Folsom Family Association, and other groups. She and Edmond continued to live in the Epping home built by her father until age and infirmity made that and other core pieces of her life no longer possible. "Considering my somewhat advanced years, I find it a bit difficult to write a letter myself," she wrote a friend a year before her death in 1974. She still had enough energy to bemoan the shuttering of her longtime school in West Epping. "I have felt quite sad to think of the old schoolhouse closed up. It seems to me that it should furnish a place where little folks could come to school once more. I am sorry that I'm not quite well enough to open it up for class!"

For his part, Edmond pursued several business ventures after leaving his job at the Navy Yard. He also got involved in local and state politics, serving as Epping's representative to the New Hampshire Legislature from 1953 to 1958 and as an Epping selectman for eighteen years. Edmond Blair "carried out his responsibilities with scrupulous integrity and excellent judgment," according to Epping's 1969 Annual Town Report, which was dedicated to Edmond, who died that year. "During the troubled times of the Great Depression, 'the needy and the homeless' found their needs supplied with tact, fairness, and unfailing kindness."

When she began keeping a journal in 1897, fifteen-year-old Mary was "anxious to see how long I shall keep it up." She managed for four decades, sometimes sporadically, but always with insight, truth, and passion. The woman "known on a time as Mary E" kept adding fresh chapters to her life's life book.

Mary Evelyn Folsom Blair died on January 14, 1973, at the age of ninety-one in West Epping, where she shaped countless young lives.

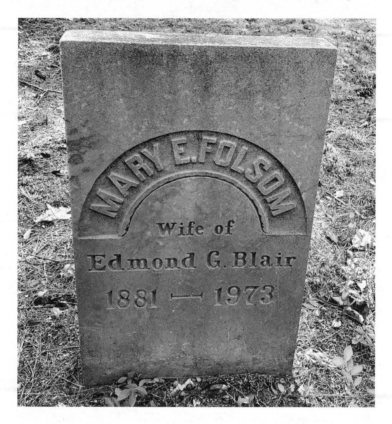

Afterword

Mary was intrigued by the possibility of communicating with the dead. So if I could somehow connect with her, what would I say? What might she want to know?

I'd start by breaking the news that while the house that her father built and in which she grew up is gone, the West Epping Rural School that she attended as a girl and from which she retired as a teacher more than sixty years later still stands. Though now a private home, the building looks nearly the same from the outside. The West Epping Friends Meeting House around the corner is also in solid structural and spiritual shape. And the Folsom land and woods about which Mary wrote such rich passages? The pastures for sheep and cattle from an earlier Folsom era have reverted to their mixed forest state. Beginning in the 1960s, Mary began selling some of her land, including a parcel to an old friend whose descendants by blood or marriage are my neighbors along Old Cart Path.

Mary would be pleased that much former Folsom land has been protected from development. Through a Life Estate Gift to the Southeast Land Trust of New Hampshire, I have deeded the original fifty-five acres that I bought from Mary's estate in 1974, plus another 54 more that I acquired since, to the Trust. The land will forever be protected and open (except to motorized vehicles). Nearby, another twenty-two acres of former Folsom property once slated to become a West Epping subdivision was turned over to the town in lieu of tax payments; it is now the John B. Folsom Conservation Area, named after Mary's nephew. whose son Neal Folsom and his wife Verna live next to it.

On September 26, 1971, ninety-year-old Mary attended the dedication of the Mary E. Folsom Blair Community Park on land where the Folsom Mill operated until the family sold it in the 1940s. (The mill building burned in 1950.). Epping youth now play baseball where logs were once stacked for milling. The plaque at the fifteen-acre park, which includes historic markers and trails and is the launching point for the annual Epping Canoe Race, reads, "In appreciation of her loving service to several generations of Epping residents, her pioneer encouragement of outdoor recreation and her embodiment of the Folsom tradition in West Epping."

Mary cared about her Folsom heritage. For a non-professional genealogist such as me, tracking the many overlapping Folsom branches—names such as Thomas, Charles, and David kept recurring—is a challenge. Mary was interested in her lineage, hosting four reunions of the Folsom Family Association, including the one at Arcady. As part of my quest, I got in contact with the West Coast family of Mary's uncle, Yellowstone explorer David E. Folsom. They and other Mary descendants I contacted were pleased to learn more about a Folsom about whom many of them knew little. Mary was, above all, a teacher, especially of history. So Neal Folsom and I felt it fitting that we donate her journals, letters, and other material to the Schlesinger Library at the Radcliffe Institute for Advanced Study in Cambridge, the successor to Radcliffe College, where Mary spent a year in 1916. With her materials properly preserved and accessible, Mary E. Folsom Blair will teach forever in a digital classroom.

Something else would please Mary. As I pursued the twisting paths of her life, I met some wonderful people who helped me connect disparate dots. In the process, some former students and others got to reconnect with each other and with key moments and places in their lives, often for the first time in decades. It was a privilege to be their past-to-present tour guide. Shortly before her death in early 2001, for example, former student Ramona Stevens visited Arcady one last time. I can still see her sitting by the dock, gazing at the lake in which she frolicked with other young Arcadians. In the course of assisting with the *Chronicle* episode about Mary in 2000, I helped reunite other old West Epping schoolmates, including Bob Tuttle and Bud Purington, who met for the first time in nearly 60 years at Bud's one-man sawmill. As a bonus, I became friends with these fine gentlemen until their deaths.

Bob and Dot Tuttle also returned to the bungalow where they spent their honeymoon. As if on a scavenger hunt through their lives, they wandered about finding inscriptions from decades past. And I will never forget the return to Arcady of two of the people most central to Mary during her life and to my quest: her nephew, Richard Hunt Perry, and Edmond's niece, Jean Pye, whose names also dot Arcady's walls and doors. A highlight from all these years, captured in a photograph in Chapter 12, was seeing Mr. Perry light up as he spotted his Aunt Mary's

26. Bob Tuttle (left), Bud Purington, and the author with one of Mary's journals.　　　—Courtesy of WCVB-TV

faded notation of his visit as one of "the small Perrys" more than eighty years earlier. I sent that photo to Mr. Perry's great granddaughter, adding another member to the Mary fan club.

Through it all, I found my own peace at Arcady and in the forests Mary once walked. "At peace" is a good description for how I feel after decades of deep diving into the life of a woman who was a meaningless name when we "met" in 1974. Something about Mary just compelled me to find and share her words and life. I am much more skeptical than Mary was about the afterlife and spiritualism, but I have found myself occasionally wondering if she and I were somehow connected.

I came to see a lot of myself in Mary. I admired her fine and honest writing, even when her vocabulary and literary acumen frequently sent me to my dictionary. I also felt a strong kinship for her preference for the natural world over the developed one, how she favored Bohemian *bonhomie* over societal standards. I especially admired her determination to get young people interested in the outdoors long before such practice became trendy. I suspect Mary would share my sadness that forests and streams and mountains have become backdrops for selfies rather than inspirations for self-discovery.

Most of all, I was drawn to Mary's independence and determination. I worked as a reporter for many years and I almost always managed to file my stories on time. But for this book, the only deadline I faced was my own mortality. Despite countless fits and oft-delayed starts, some of Mary's persistence finally rubbed off on me.

Mary liked to record special "days to be remembered." She'd have really liked a perfect fall day in 2020 when the granddaughter and great grandson of Anne Reed—Mary's precious Anne of Arcady— joined me at the bungalow. We sat on the same porch where Anne and Mary contentedly took in the lake's "sunlight and shadow and silvery nights and flitting fogs." It's only fitting for this book to close with words by Mary. In 1902, she ended a poem this way:

> Now fare you well
> Much will I tell
> Next time I write a line to thee
> My love I send.
>   'Tis from a friend.
> Known on a time as Mary E.

Acknowledgements

Some wonderful guides and collaborators, from Mary's time as well as my own, helped me to piece together the rich life and fine words of Mary E. Folsom Blair.

The first direction came nearly fifty years ago, when Epping historian Madelyn Williamson lent me the first of Mary's journals. Much more recently, Joy True, the Epping Historical Society's current president, whose husband Forrest was one of Mary's students, has offered frequent assistance. Others who knew Mary—relatives, former students, 4-H colleagues, friends (upper and lower case)— shared their memories as well as letters and other material, including many of the photographs that appear in this book. Most of those Mary contemporaries are gone now; this book is a tribute to them.

Janice and Bill Jassmond, the current owners and guardians of Arcady, gave me full access to the charmed bungalow, which they have preserved—in spirit and structure—much as Mary left it, despite the mounting pressures of modernity and taxes. Janice, whose grandmother Mildred Brown was Mary's girlhood schoolmate and lifelong friend, offered personal insights and perspective and was an especially stalwart supporter, especially when I thought I'd hit another dead end. Mary's grand-nephew Neal Folsom has been another fellow traveler on my journey to his great aunt.

Also high on the stalwart list is Brenda Wineapple, with whom I grew up in Haverhill, Mass. I wish I had a fraction of Brenda's ability to so lucidly chronicle key people and periods of American history. Judy Mears remains as loyal, thoughtful, thorough, and grammatically correct as she was in 1968, when she recruited me to the *Tufts Weekly* and a life in journalism. Others who reviewed drafts, offered comments, or helped in other ways include Jim Rurak, Susan Carey, Sol Gittleman, Donald Gropman, and Carl Carlsen. My brother Bill Primack also had good suggestions. Photographer and friend Frank Siteman helped make some old images come alive. John Wooding gave the manuscript a careful read (Joan would have approved) and steered me to Loom Press and its founder Paul Marion, who ably steered this final leg of my long road to this book.

Appendix 1
Maps

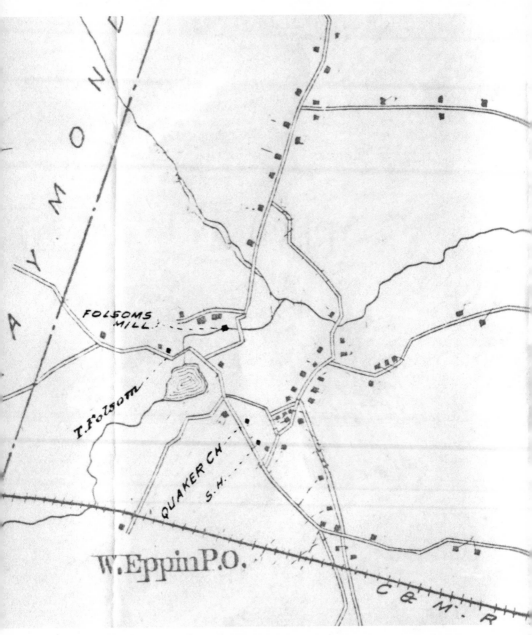

The 1892 *Town and City Atlas* of New Hampshire shows the centers of Mary Folsom Blair's West Epping universe. She was born in the house labeled "T. Folsom" in 1881 and lived there with her husband from 1918 until her death in 1973. The map also shows the family's "Folsoms Mill," Mary's schoolhouse ("S.H."). and the Quaker Meeting House ("Quaker Ch"). — *Map courtesy of the Epping Historical Society.*

Mary spent most of her life in Epping except for her years teaching in Massachusetts and studying at Radcliffe College in Cambridge. She spent summers at Arcady, her lakeside bungalow in Nottingham, N.H. She and Edmond Blair were married in Portsmouth in 1918.

Appendix 2

Mary's Presentation About the Quakers

(This is the full text of Mary's 1911 journal entry about the Quakers, excerpted in Chapter 13.).

Given for the Alliance Jan. 18
The Quakers

When I tell you of the Quakers I must tell you of a generation long gone by. If the ones that I had known had not outlived by many years their allotted three score and ten, I should not be able to give you these impressions derived from the vivid memories of childhood.

The Quaker of ye olden time has left us, and his descendants have so fallen into the ways of the world's people that there is no perceptible difference between them.

You may read in the pages of history an account of their origin and you may study their creed at your leisure from the 4th, 5th, and 6th chapters of Matthew, but these things do not give you a picture of their daily lives nor of the quant and curious customs that have made them a separate and peculiar people.

When we see good things that they advocated we would wonder why Quakerism hasn't become more dominant. The answer lies in the fact that their very doctrine of divine inspiration forbade the urging of their creed upon any individual who felt no prompting of the spirit towards it. Moreover in their avoidance of frivolity and worldliness they shut out many a harmless joy and irreverent diversion, the rightful inheritance of youth and their children sought elsewhere these natural rights. They preached a great simplicity of dress manners and speech, a broad charity towards other men, a severe uprightness of living, and they practiced their own preaching.

They were pioneers in so many great movements. We see them freeing their slaves a hundred years before the civil war, holding that no man had a right to hold in bondage his fellow man. The prison door of many an English debtor swung open to the sweet voice of Elizabeth Fry, that type of England's worthiest womanhood. At a time when every good Orthodox brought out his best West Indies or Santa Cruz for his minister's bodily refreshment, the Quakers advocated temperance. They were many years ahead of their times. In fact, we haven't quite caught up with them yet. Today the cry of the suffragette is loud in the land. They are appealing for rights held by the fair Quakeress for the last two centuries and a half for the society has ever recognized that where woman is not the superior she is the equal of man.

Loftiest of all visions, the Quaker prophet has ever dreamed of a day when the bugles of battle shall blow the marches of universal peace and every court of arbitration in the world today sees a partial realization of that vision.

Their greatest contribution to the faith of the world has been the doctrine of the Inner light divine inspiration, the belief that God speaks as directly to the children of men today as he ever did to Abraham or Moses. They listened very closely to this voice of the spirit, so closely that "I fancy but thinly the veil intervened" between the material and the spiritual world and they became dreamers of dreams and seers of visions. Thru all their sane philosophy of life and religion runs this vein of mysticism that seems more an inheritance of the Orient than a product of western materialism. You will remember how cleverly Gilbert Parker combines the two in "the Weavers" and how David's belief in the inspiration of the spirit is supplemented by Eastern fatalism.

It was this very belief in the guidance of the divine Spirit that set them at variance with their times. The Catholic held the Pope as an authority on all subjects. The Protestant believed that in his Bible had been written the last word of the laws of righteousness. The Friend found in his own heart, guided by the Inner Light, the knowledge of right and wrong and it was for this belief that he was whipped and pilloried, branded and banished and hung.

I think that many of my most vivid memories center around the little white meeting house on the plains. When I was a wee bit of a maid I used to go there with my grandparents or my father and the other good Friends who met on every First Day and sometimes on Fifth Days to worship God according to their own quaint customs. The little white meeting house still stands, plain and solid and substantial, fitting type of the men and women who worshipped within its walls. Its interior is very plain. There are no rare and costly windows thru which the mellow light may fall, no graceful arch, no solemn organ tones, only the clean white walls, the glympse of God's own sky thru the high windows and the solemn stillness save for the murmur of the wind in the great pines outside, or the lilting song of a bird. More often than not the stillness was unbroken, yet in that hour of silent meditation every man and woman found strength to bear manfully and patiently and with much courage the burdens of life and in that simple meeting place was an atmosphere of reverence that is not always present in costly temples.

Perhaps you have never seen the interior of a Quaker meeting house. Across the back where in other churches we find the altar or pulpit there is a platform raised several steps above the floor and with a railing separating it from the rest of the meeting house. A long seat runs its entire length. This is the high-facing seat where the elders and ministers sit. It is the duty of the elders to keep a careful eye, and ear on the ministers, to be sure that their doctrines are sound, to see that they act with circumspection and to admonish them if there seems to be any need. The ministers are those who are moved frequently by the spirit to preach and so had been appointed by the society. Frequently they were very young hence the need of a restraining hand from the elders.

Down in the level of the floor was another row of facing seats where might sit more elders or, as a sign of esteem, elderly people who had not been appointed elders.

The next characteristic of a friends' meeting house is a partition about three feet high running thru the middle and dividing the men's side from the women's. A sliding shutter can be rolled down to meet this partition thus completely separating the two parts. This is used when there is a business meeting and the men and women wish to consider matters separately. After they are well considered, delegates are sent from each side to the other to announce the mind of their meeting.

It is on such occasions that the intentions of marriage are announced. The demure maiden, supported by a friend of her own sex, meets her intended, similarly supported in the hall outside, and the quartette proceeds to the men's side where they take their places on the facing seats in a solemn stillness. After a few minutes meditation the couple rise and the man announces, "I, John Smith, intend marriage with Friend Mary Brown on such and such a date." The Friend Mary Brown declares her intention, and after a little further meditation they betake themselves to the women's side and go all over it again. The marriage may be held at any time or place appointed, at home, weekday meeting or monthly meeting, and is witnessed by delegates appointed by the monthly meeting who sign the certificate. The ceremony is very simple. The man rising, takes the woman by the hand and says, "Friends, I take this my Friend, Mary Brown, promising to be unto her a faithful and affectionate husband, until Death doth us separate." In like manner she makes her declaration. The certificate certifies that in this manner John Smith did say so-and-so and adds that hence forth Mary Brown consents to be called by his name—if she does consent. Bride and groom sign their names, as do all present, and the marriage is consummated. There are slightly different forms. The spirit may move them to make some slight variation.

The ceremony is beautiful in its simplicity and the vows to be faithful and affectionate made to each other in solemn dignity are well kept. But says a sweet old Quakeress "Thee knows dear child, it was a trying moment when I rose by John's side in the men's meeting and announced my intentions. I was much perturbed in spirit."

At home the meeting has always been so small since my remembrance that we have used only one side, the wide aisle dividing the men from the women. I used to sit well back and watch them come in. My great-aunt was tall and stately and used to move majestically to the high-facing seats, her heavy skirt sweeping the floor, her snowy kerchief folded in three folds in each side with mathematical precision, and her lace cap, silk bonnet, and outer shawl not daring to move one jot from their appointed place. I can remember my grandfather and my grandmother, this great aunt and another great great aunt, all well over their eighties, sitting on the high facing seats in solemn and dignified array and very imposing they seemed to me. The "young folks" of sixty and upwards were on the lower facing seats.

More often than not as I have said, the meeting was a silent one, for unless there happened to be a visiting friend present the Spirit seldom moved. However I remember well one First Day a number of the World's people visited the quiet little meeting place and to their unaccustomed ideas the silence seemed strange and the plain costumes funny and the seats very uncomfortable. So their behavior became somewhat unseemly and the spirit moved my grandfather to arise and deliver a somewhat stirring homily on the evils of curiosity, taking for his text 'What went ye out for to see.' The soothing effect on the world's people was quite marked.

It was always a great mystery to me how the elders knew when it was time to close the meeting. No one ever looked at a watch, but at precisely the same moment the elders on the upper and lower facing seats turned toward each other and solemnly shook hands, the movement was repeated in every seat and the meeting was over. Conversation became lively, with such remarks as, "Evelyn, has thee heard from Friend Susan Brown lately?", or, "Friend George Beede, thee and Ruth must come home to dinner." George and Ruth had eight children and a dinner invitation was no small matter. It meant a great deal in those days but Quaker hospitality was always equal to it. They went on the principal of "What I have give I thee. If ye are good folk, ye won't complain and if ye are not good folk, it is good enough for ye."

Monthly meetings were very important events. They were something like the modern conferences. So many monthly meetings made up a quarterly. To Amesbury quarterly belonged Amesbury, Pittsfield, West Newbury, Seabrook and West Epping. There comes clearly to my mind the murmur of a sweet May morning several years ago, when, leaving my little school-house , I drove with my good father over winding country roads, past apple orchards, heavy with the bloom of pink and white, to the quaint little old academy town of Exeter. From there our route lay thru the Hamptons, our destination Amesbury and the Friends Quarterly meeting which is held there on the third Fifth day of every Fifth month, or, in the language of the world's people, the third Thursday in May. Quarterly meeting is more important than the monthly meeting. It is a court as well as a religious meeting. Marriages may be made, disputes are settled, members are disciplined if need be. The court of final appeal was the yearly meeting. Disputes were rarely carried outside into the national courts. The monthly meeting also had its business side but I know little of it.

The social side was more familiar. For days and days before monthly meeting Grandmother swept and dusted and cooked. The dresser shelves were decorated with wonderful arrays of pies, the prides of the poultry yards were baked and boiled and most fearfully garnished, the hams were hung in the smoke box, the cake trunk was lined with dark red spice cakes, and sombre coffee cakes and light and fluffy Berwick sponges, to say nothing of cookies and cookies, and doughnuts galore, enough to feed a regiment. On the great day grandmother donned her best bonnet and shawl and she and my grandfather drove off in the heavy old chaise to meeting. When they returned they brought back all the friends that had not wandered to other havens. There used to be fifteen or twenty in the old days return for dinner, sweet faced old ladies in their best silk gowns and finest lace caps, somewhat stern faced men in straight-colared coats and broad brimmed hats.

There was one old Quaker from Candia who used to dress in drab thruout, drab coat and trousers and hat. He was a Hicksite Quaker and was plainer and more severe in dress and manner and speech than the orthodox or Wilburites. In belief the Hicksites were Unitarians. Friend George Beede's father always wore black or white or gray clothes, believing it to be sinful and unworthy to wear dyed goods. The black came from the wool of his black lambs, the white from the white fleece and he obtained a most sober and godly gray mixing the two. The dinner always began with a silent blessing. That was another great puzzle to my childish mind. I never could understand how they knew to leave off the blessing and begin the eating. I even watched for surreptitious signs under the table but I was never able to detect any.

After dinner, if it was in the summer time, grandfather greatly delighted in leading his guests out into the garden. All the friends that I have known loved flowers. It was their one way of expressing their love for color and beauty. This old time garden would have made a fitting story setting. A brook came dashing into it, under an old arch, leaping gayly down a cascade and following its walled in way across it. Gray, moss grown planks formed foot bridges here and there a somewhat uncertain pathway for the dancing feet of a child.

Across the brook was a low terrace backed by a high bank stoned in and made doubly high by a picket fence on which the grape vines ran in wild confusion. There was no set order in this garden. Flower and vegetable and herb grew wherever the sun or soil suited them. In the early spring time long rows of scarlet tulips lifted their cups to the sun, the snow-drops bloomed under the window, the purple and white lilacs loaded the heavy air with fragrance. The dear white daffys, my mother's favorite, pushed its green shoots up thru the moist earth, and a feathery bell like flower grew very near them. Hundreds of Ladies Delights grew up in the strawberry bed. In June the roses bloomed galore, their coming heralded by the opening of the cinnamon roses, always sturdy and self-reliant, then the ivory white ones, the pale yellow, the prairie rose, the tiny white Scotch ones with oh <u>such</u> prickly stems, the queenly damask, the blush rose and old-fashioned single rose, both beautiful in their buds but falling too soon from their flower.

Pride of my grandfather's heart was the big seven sister that stood in the middle of the vegetable patch and bore its hundred blossoms at a time. Later in the summer, the peonies bloomed and beds of pansies and portaluccas, zinnias and moss pinks and petunias held sway. The stately stock flourished in close company with beds of sage, and snake root, balm and wormwood. Against the feathery asparagus stood clumps of gorgeous tiger lilies. At one season of the year the bed of the brook glowed with the gold of buttercups, so double that their blossoms made a yellow ball. There was no time in the year when some fascinating green thing couldn't be found within these garden walls.

If monthly meetings happened to come in winter, the early twilight drew us to the great fireplace where the flames roared up the chimney and the candles sputtered on the mantle. The light shone on placid faces, on snowy caps and kerchiefs of the women and the white locks of the old men. The subdued click of needles kept up a pleasant accompaniment to the exchange of wit and wisdom, quaint legends and thrilling adventures.

Oh such stories as they told. There was that one of the last wolf hunt when the great gray wolf that made her den between the mountains and the lake had come down and wrought such havoc in the sheepfold. Since nothing is impossible to the imagination of a child I used to cuddle down under the blankets and altho ¾ of a century had passed since that exciting day I heard the gray wolf howl in every shriek of the wind and shivered most delicious horrors at the thought of it ranging thru the dark pines back of the house.

Or there might be some wonderful tale or signs or vision or warning or thrilling adventures of pioneer days in the West, retold from the stirring letters of sons and daughters who had braved the perils of the wilderness. The element of humor was not lacking for those old

Quakers dearly loved a joke, especially if it hinged at all upon their own peculiarities.

The signs and warnings always interested me. Grandfather, who was of an investigating frame of mind, always had a logical explanation for everything much to grandmother's perturbation. Why, just think of that forewarning she had received when it was borne in upon her one morning to rise early and bake pies and cake and bread and meat and doughnuts and cookies, and come night time nine visiting Friends had come to stay all night. Grandfather would say, "Well, Soviah, thee knows it was quarterly meeting at Amesbury and this was always the half way place between Amesbury and Pittsfield. Don't thee think that had something to do with thy warning?"

Well, what if it did. There was the time when Charles lay desperately ill at Friend's Boarding School, and she had heard his voice calling, "Mother, Mother" in the middle of the night and she had made ready to go before ever the message came. That wasn't due to its being Quarterly meeting at Amesbury was it. Grandfather was always discreetly silent here as far as words were concerned, but he had a most sceptical cough.

Those old days are gone never to be recalled save in memory. As I have read or heard quoted some quaint legend or homily tale of our dear Quaker poet, I can well imagine their soiree or inspiration, and say with him henceforward listen as we will. The voices of that hearth are still. Look where we may the world o'er. Those lighted faces smile no more. We turn the pages that they read. Their written words we linger over. But in the sun they cast no shade. No voice is heard, no sign is made. No step is on the conscious floor. But love will dream and faith will hold. Since he, who knows our need, is just. That somehow, somewhere meet we must. Who has not learned in hours of fact? The truth to Flesh and Sense unknown. That life is ever Lord of Death. And Love can never lose its run.

Index

A Note on the Author

Photo: Frank Siteman

Phil Primack has been a reporter, journalism instructor, and freelance writer, editor, and consultant. After graduating from Tufts University in 1970, he worked for eastern Kentucky's weekly, *The Mountain Eagle*. He was a staff reporter for *The Boston Herald* and his freelance pieces appeared in the *Boston Globe*, *New York Times*, *Washington Post*, the *Nation*, *Columbia Journalism Review* and other publications. Primack has also taught at several colleges and universities.

Primack, who earned a Master of Public Administration degree from Harvard University in 1987, has been a policy adviser to elected officials and state and federal agencies and has consulted for a wide range of foundations and other non-profit organizations. His book, *New England Country Fair* (Globe Pequot Press, 1981), which arose from his years working on the midway of a traveling carnival, "captures the fine feel of small-town Yankee America gently showing off," wrote Studs Terkel. Primack continues to pursue writing projects from his home in Medford, Mass.